IN THE GARLIC

To be in the garlic, estar en el ajo:
to be clued up, to know the score

Valerie Collins & Theresa O'Shea

IN THE GARLIC

Published by Ediciones Santana, S.L.
Apartado 41, 29650 Mijas-Pueblo (Málaga), Spain
Tel. (0034) 952 48 58 38 Fax. (0034) 952 48 53 67
E-Mail info@santanabooks.com

Copyright © 2006 Valerie Collins & Theresa O'Shea
Illustrations Copyright © 2006 Dan Pearce

Designed by Imigiz S.L. (www.imigiz.com)

Printed in Spain by Gráficas San Pancracio, S.L.
ISBN-13: 978-84-89954-59-5
ISBN-10: 84-89954-59-3
Depósito Legal: MA-1.493/2006

Between them the authors of this book have more than 50 years' experience of the joys and tribulations of living in Spain.

Born in Manchester, England, but for many years based in Barcelona, Valerie Collins has worked extensively as a translator and writer. She was first hooked on Spain when she enjoyed a holiday in Benidorm at the age of 15. She later married Enric, a Catalan lawyer, raised a family (she now has two grown-up sons, Eduard and Robert) and became an expert on negotiating Spanish/Catalan red tape.

Theresa O'Shea, a freelance journalist and writer, lives in a small village in the Axarquía district of Málaga province. Originally from near Rugby, England, she travelled in Asia and North America before taking up a teaching post in Spain. She intended to stay a year or so to brush up her Spanish before heading off for more travels. But meeting Francisco, from Andalusia, helped persuade her to make her home in Spain.

ACKNOWLEDGEMENTS

My thanks to co-author and friend Valerie. Her support, erudition and expert feedback, especially during the early years of my writing career, boosted my confidence and instilled in me the need to always strive for excellence.

A huge thanks to all my friends who showed interest in the project, offered suggestions, and listened patiently to my blow-by-blow progress reports.

A special gracias to Sandra M, without whose generosity and trust this book would never have been written. Also to Miranda Innes, for her help and encouragement.

Finally, a big thank you to my parents for their unfailing support, and to Guengo (aka, Francisco) who puts up with my writer's temperament with far more sweetness and light than I deserve.

— Theresa O'Shea

Thanks above all to co-writer Theresa, sounding board, shoulder to cry on, amiga and compañera for enough years that I can't imagine life without her. Working with her has immeasurably enriched my writing.

A number of good friends have been unstinting in their encouragement and support. I'm especially grateful to Maria-José Anía, Shari Nilson, Judy Reeves (who got me writing again after my husband Enric died), Maggie Pannikar and John Sarginson, whose enthusiasm sparked this project into life and often revived flagging spirits. Special thanks go to Graham and Heather Lovegrove and to Paquita Cíller, supportive presences in my life for so long. I would like to pay tribute to Gwen Mosedale, one of my oldest friends in Barcelona and a true veteran of the struggle with Spanish (and Catalan) bureaucracy, who died just before this book went to press.

Finally, to my sons Eduard and Robert and my mother Irene Collins, thank you from the heart.

— Valerie Collins

JOINT ACKNOWLEDGEMENTS

We would like to thank Suzan Davenport (and all at *Costa del Sol News and Costa Blanca News*) for publishing our column and for her encouragement.

A big thanks to everybody at Santana for being so open to our ideas and suggestions, to David Baird for his eagle-eyed editing, to Dan Pearce for his fabulous drawings, to Miranda Innes for her kind words, and to Phill and Fiona, who captured the spirit of *In The Garlic* by giving the book its fun, fresh look.

Dedicated, with love, to the people of Spain.

FOREWORD

This book has been put together by two women who came to Spain in their 20s to learn the language and have stayed ever since. While they definitely do not deny the difficulties, there is an exuberant sense that, having made the leap, they celebrate more often than not and would live nowhere else. *In The Garlic* is a brilliantly helpful and witty guide to surviving and thriving in Spain written by two who know.

In addition to offering practical advice the book is full of fascinating and wonderfully quotable research. For weeks after I read it, I found myself recounting anecdotes and regaling friends with interesting snippets of information — about the Himno Nacional, Chupa Chups and *futbolín* for a start. Thanks to In the Garlic I finally understand the mysteries of *el puente,* which would have saved me no end of grief had I been less ignorant, and I have discovered that I have my own language, Mirandese, otherwise known, somewhat offensively, as Bable. This book is an entertaining companion, holding your hand through the bad bits and leavening the initiate's disasters with wry humour. I just wish it had been around to cheer and advise when I trawled through every mistake a novice can make.

In the stress of moving to a new country you may well be mesmerised by the crushing juggernaut of bureaucracy. You will find yourself waiting endlessly in unruly queues for some rubber stamp to ratify some incomprehensible form — and you will never have brought the correct documents, ever, be it to legitimise your car, pay unexpected taxes or get your toe bandaged. As you will discover in the pages of this invaluable and cheering book, the phenomenon has a name: the Law of Falta Uno. I survived this stage by reading. I have never been so well read as when trying to sort out the simple mechanics of everyday life in Spain. You, however, can cut out years of just bumbling along by consulting this book. Not only does it tell you loads of stuff you need to know, it will also make you laugh and, crucially, it will make you feel less alone. There is nothing lonelier than waving farewell to friends and family, burning your nice, manageable British boats, and fetching up in a place where you don't know the rules, can't speak the language and there always seems to be someone shouting at you.

Fortunately, Theresa and Valerie are at hand to encourage you through any grisly moments. And one thing you know: waking up to sunshine, sitting out beneath a silver moon while seduced by wafts of lemon blossom and jasmine, watching grannies salsa far into the night with wide-eyed grand-daughters in spotted flamenco flounces...all this beats anything that Basildon has to offer. The Spanish are kind, the bureaucracy impenetrable but — with the exception of Telefónica — they do not cut off vital services, and Spain is a joyous, happening place to live.

— Miranda Innes

PRONUNCIATION

Recently an Australian friend of ours who speaks hardly any Spanish left some written instructions for visitors staying in his flat in Barcelona. Under "Transport" he wrote: "Tarhetta - from vending machines at station." David knew the word *tarjeta* (card) but not how to write it in Spanish, so he wrote it in English just as he pronounced it. That's what we've done in this book. Our "tarhetta" style transcriptions are simply a guideline for uttering something comprehensible — or, hopefully, understanding it when uttered at you. We have confined ourselves to those words and expressions which our experience suggests give the most trouble. For an accurate guide to pronouncing Spanish, readers should consult a reputable language book or course, or study with a qualified teacher.

Note re words in bold type: more information on this subject can be found under the appropriate heading.

Abecedario The alphabet. Also a booklet or chart to help children learn to say and write their ABC (ah bay thay). You will see that in your Spanish dictionary there are 27 letters: the 26 letters of the universal Latin alphabet, plus the specifically Spanish ñ. If your child is learning to read at school, however, he or she will bring home an *abecedario* with 29 letters — including **ch** and **ll** (pronounced el-ye). **Ch** and **ll** are, in fact, digraphs, i.e. they are composed of two letters to represent a single sound. According to the Dictionary of the **Real Academia Española** (DRAE), they have been considered letters in their own right since 1803. However, in 1994, under pressure from UNESCO and other international organisations, the association of all the Real Academias of Spanish-speaking countries agreed to sort **ch** and **ll** as ordinary pairs of letters. Thus, in dictionaries and encyclopedias, instead of having their own chapters, they now take their place within the "c" and "l" sections respectively. But if you should ever reach the last question on the *Who Wants to be a Millionaire?* quiz show and the question is: "How many letters are there in the Spanish aphabet?", the answer is: "The same as there were 200 years ago, 29."

Abono Be careful: *abono* doubles as a season ticket and fertiliser. If you travel on urban public transport you can save money by buying an *abono* (just to confuse things, in some places called a **bono**) of 10 tickets. The verb *abonar* means both to pay and to spread fertiliser. Where there's muck there's money and all that.

Agosto Spain is closed. Do not attempt to buy a house, get a new kitchen put in, renew your driving licence, make an

13

insurance claim, see a doctor, give birth... While 95 per cent of the population is on holiday, those who work in the tourist industry are busy "making their August", i.e. making a killing/bomb/packet. The expression *hacer el agosto* originally referred to harvest time, in particular to the casual labourers hired during this period who, in a bumper year, could make enough money to see them through the winter.

Ajo Garlic. Think in terms of heads, rather than individual cloves and, if you are of a Dracula-like disposition, emigrate elsewhere. The Spanish put masses of the stuff in and on just about everything: they chop it up by the bucket-load and fry it with green beans, sizzle it with mushrooms and shower it on tomato salads. They rub single cloves on toast, drop whole cloves into lentil stews, and use several thousand heads to make *sopa de ajo*, garlic soup. Oh, and they beat it into a pulp, adding olive oil drop by drop until it forms *alioli,* the most heavenly, blow-your-mouth-off sauce on earth. Idiomatically speaking, to be in the garlic, *estar en el ajo*, means to be clued up, to know the score. Which is, of course, exactly what you'll be by the time you've read this book.

Alcalde Mayor. Even the tiniest middle-of-nowhere *pueblo* has one. And, if no-one else fancies the job, it's not unusual to find a civic-minded 18-year-old or unschooled octogenarian holding office. Or even a well-integrated, linguistically competent chap or chappess from northern Europe.

Almuerzo From the Arabic article *al* and the Latin for "bite", *morsus* (morsel). Officially means lunch but is also used to refer to a substantial mid-morning snack, also known (by us, at any rate) as *"el segundo desayuno"*: the Second Breakfast.

Alquiler/alquilar *Alquiler* is what you pay while you're looking for that dream property: rent. Almost impossible not to confuse with the verb, *alquilar* (to rent). Renting accommodation is fraught with difficult terms. You are the *inquilino*, the tenant, and your landlord/landlady is the *casero/casera*. Standard practice is to pay a one or two-month *fianza*, or deposit. Can't be bothered with the *alquiler*? You can always find an empty house and become an *okupa* — a squatter.

15

Alta This word, which must be one of the most-used in Spain today, takes most of us years to figure out because we keep thinking it's something to do with *alto* as in tall. No. *El alta* is a signing-up for a service or some kind of list or register. *Darse de alta* means to put oneself on an official list, to register, to join, to become a member, to enrol, to enlist. It can refer to registering a vehicle, signing up for Internet access, a mobile phone contract or satellite TV, taking out an insurance policy, registering with the social security or the tax people. Healthwise, the *alta* is a discharge from hospital, or the official paper from your doctor saying you are fit again. Be warned: service companies in every sector are fighting to sign you up. Among their enticements may be *alta gratis* or *gratuito,* which means you don't pay any sign-up charge. But watch the small print. The easier it is to get on a list, the more difficult it is to get off (or rather down – *darse de* **baja**).

Ambulatorio This one had Valerie foxed for years, as she had the good fortune never to have to go to one. She imagined it to be some sort of circulating library we used to have back home, or possibly a Red Cross tent with people ambling in and out in frayed dressing gowns and carpet slippers. In fact, it is an out-patient clinic.

Amigo In her wonderful memoir of her life in Spain, *A Woman Unknown*, Lucia Graves mentions how a friend called the Spanish political system of the Sixties an *amigocracia:* nothing, she explains, could be achieved without influential friends, even getting a phone installed in months instead of years depended on whom you knew (and you thought a few weeks was unacceptable!). Is Spain still *una amigocracia?* To a large extent, yes. Another coinage, this one more derogatory, is *amiguismo*, or "friendism", i.e. giving cushy jobs, contracts, etc. to your friends. In Spain, the best way to get things done is through *amigos*, or more broadly, word of mouth. There's no special word for networking in Spanish because that's the natural way things have always been done here. Forget the Yellow Pages and get a little help from your friends and their friends and their friends' friends...

16

Amortización Repayment (of a loan). Unlike UK banks which now use plain English (pay in, take out etc.), Spanish ones, despite their ultra-modern image, still revel in the long-winded.

Andaluz The powers that be (the Council of Education and Science of the Junta de Andalucía) have decided that *andaluz* is not a dialect, but a "variety" of standard Castilian. The differences between the two are mostly to do with accent, the wholesale swallowing of word endings (and even middles), and the unintelligible rendering of the names of international film stars. Plurals lose their esses (*la casa* and *las casas* sound virtually the same), the "d" disappears with alarming frequency, especially in past participles (*hablao*, instead of *hablado*, *comío* instead of *comido*, etc.); and esses and other consonants in the middle of words get aspirated (the chap who used to deliver Theresa's pizzas announced his arrival through the intercom: "Piha ehpreh" (Pizza Express). The other defining features of *andaluz* are *el seseo* and *el ceceo*. In some areas of Andalusia (mostly the north) people tend to pronounce "s", "z" and soft "c" as "s" — *seseo;* while in the south, a lisper's paradise, the three sounds are pronounced like the "th" in think — *ceceo*. Thus, *necesario* (in standard Castilian, *nethesario*) becomes either *nesesario* or *nethethario*.

All very interesting, but hardly an obstacle to understanding, or is it? Theresa has lived in Andalusia for nine years but when her Malaga yoga instructor asked her to visualise *"una roza (ro-tha) blanca"* (a white something or other) during a meditation, she was completely in the dark. So she improvised and conjured up a white rock. "How did it go?" he asked, when the meditation was over. "Great," Theresa replied, "but what's a *roza*?" Laughter all round. She had failed to understand the simplest of words: *una rosa*, a rose. Even Valerie, who's lived in Spain, albeit Catalonia, since forever, was totally flummoxed when Theresa's Andalusian partner asked her if she would like *"pi-hto con huevoh"* for lunch. Blank face. Repetition. Puzzled, slightly annoyed face. More repetition. And eventually a confused: "No, I wouldn't!" Theresa translated — for both their sakes. Francisco was asking her if she wanted *pisto con huevos* (a sort of fine ratatouille with fried eggs) and she thought he was asking her if she wanted "willy with balls" — *pito* is a friendly word for penis and *huevos* (eggs) is slang for bollocks. Basically, you haven't got a chance.

Andorra Very long and very crowded duty-free shopping street running through the mountains between Spain and

France. Actually Andorra is a mini-country, officially called the Principality of Andorra, an autonomous parliamentary co-principality whose titular co-princes are the president of France and the bishop of the border town of La Seu d'Urgell in Spain (a quaint arrangement that has endured since 1278). Andorra has great ski resorts and is also a major tax haven, although this status is now threatened by EU legislation such as the recent Savings Tax Directive (basically, if you are resident in the EU, you will now have to pay tax on the interest on your money stashed away in so-called third countries such as Andorra). Catalan is the only official language of the Principat d'Andorra, but the Andorrans (70,549 of them according to a recent estimate) also speak Castilian and French.

APA Asociación de Padres de Alumnos. The equivalent of the PTA (Parents and Teachers' Association) but without the teachers. If you belong to the APA, your children qualify for hugely subsidised extra-curricular activities such as karate, drawing, and *manualidades* (arts and crafts). If your child's school has an APMA rather than an APA, don't worry: the extra letter is part of the current wave of political correctness and stands for *madres*. Apart from meaning fathers in particular, *padres* also means parents in general — at least that's what men have always thought. Then along come these stroppy *mujeres* complaining that the word excludes them...

Apellido Have you ever had to fill in a Spanish form or provide the authorities with info, and been asked for your *segundo apellido* (second surname)? There's no point in getting into unwinnable arguments about how Brits have only one surname (which incites incomprehension and, often, deep, wordless pity), and these days, with the influx of assorted immigrants, expats, Erasmus students and so on from all over the world, form-fillers are in fact getting more accustomed to people only having one. If pressed, or if the computer refuses to process your form without it, just fill in the box with your mother's maiden name. Or at least put a dash, unless you want to end up like an acquaintance of Valerie's, Jeffrey Barton, aka Jay Barton Barton as Vodafone christened him.

A lot of people think (and some of them even state it categorically on their websites) that Spaniards have double-barrelled names "because the woman adds her husband's surname to her own". Wrong. And, if you think about it, this doesn't explain anything anyway, because *everyone* has two surnames, not just married women. The official name a Spanish person carries for life on his/her ID card consists of the father's surname followed by the mother's (recent legislation allows one to reverse this order and a single parent can now register a child with both his/her own surnames.) Spanish women never officially have a married name. For example: Vicente Santillana Pérez and María Velasco García (married or not) have a son called Juan and register him in the normal way, so his official name is Juan Santillana Velasco. When Juan Santillana Velasco grows up and has a daughter, Ana, with Elena Castro Molina, then the daughter will be called Ana Santillana Castro. Officially. Unofficially, a woman who feels her *apellidos* are boring or undistinguished has options. María Velasco García may call herself:

María Velasco de Santillana (sounds brilliant actually)
María Velasco García de Santillana (even more brilliant)
Señora (de) Santillana
Señora de Santillana Pérez

This custom can be a boon if your foreign apellido, like that of Valerie (Collins), is conducive to embarrassing jokes. Catalans say (stressing the last syllable) "CoolYEENS!", often with a barely concealed snigger/giggle (collons, pronounced coolYONS, means balls). Valerie's friend Gwen Mosedale, however, has happily adopted her Spanglish surname, Mosadella, which of course sounds like a rather classy Italian wine. Theresa doesn't even bother saying her surname any more (even though there is a prestigious Spanish musician called Paloma O'Shea). She just spells it out to avoid the confusion and the jokes. There are no Spanish words that start with, or include "sh", so "sh" is pronounced "s". O'Shea sounds exactly like "o sea" (meaning "in other words") and is pronounced oSAYa. "Aha," people exclaim, as if they're the first ones to ever spot the pun, "O sea, eres O sea. (In other words, you're 'in other words')."

By the way, if you still do pre-digital things like sending letters or cards, when writing to a family, you don't need to take up the whole envelope. Just put: Familia Santillana Velasco

API Agente de la Propiedad Inmobiliaria. A real estate agent. Valerie still finds it difficult to use this acronym because api is the Catalan word for celery.

20

Aranés One of Spain's minority languages which everyone forgets about as it's only spoken by around 5,000 people in the Vall d'Aran (Aran Valley) in the Pyrenees of Catalonia, where it's co-official with both Catalan and Castilian. If you can't place the Vall d'Aran, it's where Baqueira Beret is located, a favourite ski resort of royals and celebs plus paparazzi, as seen in the pages of ¡Hola! magazine. (And, for your pub quiz, it is also the source of the River Garonne, which flows through the famed Bordeaux vineyards and into the Dordogne). In 1979 the Catalan Statute of Autonomy recognised the traditional organisation of the valley, and in 1990 the Catalan parliament passed a law giving it a special regime with the reinstatement of its Conselh Generau (General Council). Aranese is a variety (strongly influenced by Aragonese and Catalan) of the Gascon dialect, which belongs to Occitan, a group of Romance languages that includes Gascon and Provençal. Regularly taught in all the valley's primary schools, it is now experiencing a renaissance.

According to a language census of 2001, around 62 per cent of the valley's population speak Aranese, 88 per cent understand it, 58 per cent can read it and 26 per cent can write it. Most Aranese are also fluent in Spanish, Catalan and French.

Arroba This is how you say the @ ("at") in email addresses in Spanish and Portuguese. *Arroba* refers both to the sign and to an old Spanish unit of weight equivalent to around 25 English pounds. Far more interesting is the current use of the sign in the battle against sexist language, where it is used to substitute the masculine "o" in nouns which refer to groups of mixed gender. So instead of writing *"los niños"* (the children), and excluding girls, and instead of writing the politically correct but long-winded *"los niños y las niñas"*, we can write *l@s niñ@s* and keep everyone happy. However, there are plenty of academics, journalists, and *ciudadan@s* (citizens) who are up in arms about all such attempts to tamper with the Spanish language. Quite how the new vowel should be pronounced is anybody's guess.

21

Aseo *Aseo* is at the politer restroom end of the toilet terminology scale. You will often see signs for *Aseos* in restaurants, bus stations, bars etc. *Aseo* actually comes from the verb *asear*, meaning to wash up, spruce up; in oldspeak, to make your toilette.

Asistenta Many middle-class families have an *asistenta* who cleans and irons, and perhaps cooks, and looks after small children and/or elderly parents. Those who work by the hour are often local mothers with school-age children. Live-in *asistentas* are no different — except they have left their children behind in Ecuador, Colombia, and other impoverished Latin American countries. Mercedes, the live-in carer of Theresa's parents-in-law, used to send all but 50 euros a month back to her family in Ecuador. Her wage supported her mother and eight children, as well as her brother and his family. Like most immigrants in domestic service, until recently she worked illegally. However, in 2005 the Socialist government made it easier for the so-called *sin papeles* (those without papers) to obtain a residence permit. Mercedes now has her *papeles.* This means she can safely leave Spain without fear of being deported on return, and in the summer of 2005, for the first time in four years, she was able to visit her family.

Atención al cliente Things are improving, slowly, but customer service in Spain still leaves much to be desired. When you need to take something back to a shop, the *Atención al cliente* desk is where you must head, armed with your receipt and a steely resolve. Just remember, the customer is always wrong.

Ático You're looking for a flat, and they tell you it's an *ático*, and you freak out when you see what they're asking. But no, you don't have to pay 1000 euros a month to enter your home via a stepladder and a trap door and share your life with cobwebby old suitcases, broken lamps, and bits of bead curtain. *Ático* is a false friend. It's the top floor, the penthouse, and *áticos* are sought after and expensive because they often have big terraces and fabulous views. On the downside, they get damp and leaky, and boiling hot in summer. To say nothing of what happens if the lift breaks down.

22

Autonomía The Spanish equivalent of home rule, or regional autonomy. It also means how many more kilometres your car will do before it runs out of petrol — at least it does on our dashboard digital thingie — and how long you can pace around shouting into a cordless phone before the battery goes dead. *Las Autonomías* refers to the **Comunidades Autónomas.**

Autonómico/a Does not refer to the hapless **autónomos** (self-employed), but means "of or pertaining to the **comunidades**

autónomas ". So, for example, we can talk about *la televisión autonómica de Galicia, la policía autonómica de Catalunya*, and so on.

Autónomo Self-employed, freelance. Until recently, *autónomos* were regarded as non-human, or possibly superhuman. They mostly fell, arms helplessly flailing, into a black hole or no man's land between employees (*empleados)* and employers (*la empresa*). *Autónomos* are forced to pay hefty social security contributions, nearly a quarter of the basic average salary established for your profession, for the dubious reward of a measly old age pension. Until recently, if an *autónomo* got sick, they could not get sick pay until they'd been sick for 15 days, by which time they'd probably recovered, gone bankrupt or even shuffled off this mortal coil.

Autopista / autovía. Motorway / dual carriageway with motorway-like characteristics. To the untrained eye, these may look the same, but *autopistas* are generally faster, have wider lanes, a wider hard shoulder and do not admit any unmotorised vehicles. Some *autovías* actually allow suicidal moped riders, cyclists, tractors, donkeys and battery-powered buggies to use the hard shoulder. But beware, when you're zooming down the slip road on your quad bike: the white-on-blue road signs for both types of road are very similar. (Spanish road signs are unanimously agreed to be "*un asunto pendiente*", a matter yet to be sorted).

Aval/Avalista Roughly translated, guarantee and guarantor. Frequently necessary to persuade banks to lend you large amounts of money, and hugely important in a country that still does half of its business under the table with barely disguised nods and winks. Many employees of small firms receive official salaries which are substantially less than their actual earnings, so often the only way to become mortgageable is with an *aval* from a propertied friend or relative. As Theresa and Francisco found out when they tried to secure a hefty loan to purchase their dream home — a traditional village house dressed up in a palette of pinks and blues and yellows and set in a labyrinth of fruit-tree-edged patios and terraces and cobbled floors inlaid with Roman-style mosaics (they just had to have it). But, with Theresa's laughably low official earnings and Francisco's short-term contract, they were sent away empty-handed by bank after bank and told to save some more. Enter the extreme good faith and generosity of an extremely good friend, who put her property on the dotted line to help them buy theirs.

AVE (Ah-vay). Is it a bird? Is it a plane? Yes and no. It's a bird and a high-speed train. AVE is an acronym of Alta Velocidad Española, and *ave* is the Spanish for bird. Operated by **RENFE**, the supertrains travel at up to 300 kph, cutting journey times in half. They also offer airline-type service and facilities, including at-your-seat dining and a half-price happy hour at the bar. Amazingly, if your "bird" arrives more than 20 minutes later than the advertised time, you are entitled to a 25 per cent refund; more than 60 minutes late and you get a total refund. Now that would be a great way to put all the Virgin/South-West/Central/the-Bits-No-one-Else-Wants companies in the UK out of business.

Two long-distance, high-speed rail services, Madrid-Sevilla, and Madrid-Zaragoza-Lleida, have been inaugurated, also the Madrid-Toledo line — and more are under construction. When they have sorted out a series of very large hiccups with tunnels, train speeds, signalling, dodgy clay and angry environmentalists, the Lleida line will extend to Barcelona. By 2010 the government hopes to have 7,000 kilometres of high-speed rail up and running, with all provincial capitals no more than four hours from Madrid and six-and-a-half hours from Barcelona. Don't hold your breath.

Ayuntamiento The town hall. Found in just about every village, town and city. Usually a stately white or honey-coloured building flanked by flags, often fronted by the *plaza mayor* and housing lots of important people and departments you need to know about, such as the Policía Municipal, to report a theft or dispute; **Empadronamiento**, to register as a resident; and Urbanismo (Town Planning), to discover the bargain plot of land you've bought has been earmarked for a new motorway. The *ayuntamiento* is also the place to find out about super-subsidised courses in aerobics, pottery, text-messaging for dummies, how to decipher a phone bill from Telefónica and so on.

Bable *La llingua propia d'Asturies y de parte de Llión, Zamora y Miranda del Douru*. Bable, also known as Asturian, Leonese and Astur-Leonese, is a Romance language spoken in some parts of Asturias, León, Zamora and Salamanca and in the area of Miranda do Douro in Portugal (where it is officially recognised as Mirandese). Yes, yet another endangered minority language that is fighting for recognition. Since 1980 much effort has been made to protect and promote Bable under the autonomous legislation, and it is an optional language in schools in Asturias. In 1994 100,000 spoke it as a first language, and 450,000 more were able to speak or understand it. While some reports claim that Asturian will be dead within two generations, the number of young people learning and using it (mainly as a written language) has substantially increased in recent years, mainly among intellectual groups and politically active Asturians and Leonese proud of their regional identity. At the end of the 20th century, the Academia de la Llingua Asturiana (based in Uviéu, aka Oviedo) made efforts to provide most of the tools needed by a language to ensure its survival: a grammar, a dictionary, and periodicals. A new generation of Asturian writers in both Asturias and León has also championed the language. These developments, and a growing Internet presence, give the Asturian-Leonese language a greater hope of survival.

Bachillerato *El bachillerato* is the final, non-compulsory phase of secondary education, lasting two years, normally between 16 and 18 years of age, the equivalent of the UK sixth form and the prerequisite for university. When Valerie's sons, Eduard and Robert, were doing el bat, as they called it (from the Catalan batxillerat), she never really got the hang of how it functioned, and was convinced that the schools made it up as they went along. Modalidades, comunes, optativas, what percentages of what marks counted towards what partial or global mark, what subjects, or parts of subjects you could or couldn't re-sit if you failed... it was a total mystery.

Research for this book, however, has made everything crystal clear -well, almost. There are four *modalidades* i.e. broad subject areas: Arts; Natural and Health Sciences; Humanities and Social Sciences; and Technology. And please note that *Artes* are Arts (painting, design, photography etc.) not what we call Arts (as in an Arts degree), which corresponds to Humanidades. Unlike A levels, however, rather than at last being left in peace to specialise in three or four favourite or best subjects, whichever *modalidad* you choose, you also have to do a pile of *materias comunes*: Castilian language and literature, co-official language (if any) of your autonomous community and literature, a foreign language, philosophy, history, P.E. and religion (voluntary). And then there are the *materias optativas* from a wider choice of optional subjects, depending on the size and resources of your school. All your marks are added up to give an all-round average mark. This represents 60 per cent of the final mark that will determine university entrance, with the marks obtained in the university entrance exams (see **Selectividad**) accounting for the other 40 per cent. Dazed and confused? Not to worry. Your teenagers, even when useless at maths like Valerie's were, will have a perfect grasp of how the *bachillerato* functions. What you do need to know, though, is that *un bachiller* is not a Bachelor of Whatever (i.e. a person with a university degree), but someone who has passed the *bachillerato*.

Baja The opposite of **alta**. You need a *baja médica* (an official sick note) in order to get sick pay, insurance money and so on. If you are *de baja*, you are off work. If you are on maternity leave, you are *de baja por maternidad*. To *darse de baja* from a service, insurance policy, etc. can be less than simple. You are required to send grovelling faxes, within X working days, containing copies of your ID to numbers that are engaged all day long. You go to the bank and stop the direct debit and then they start sending you bills by post, and you try to phone. When you phone (a euro-guzzling 902 number, we might add) you're on permahold all day, and then you get a threatening letter from a debt-collecting agency in Madrid... Be warned: read the small print, and find out before you do the *alta* what the procedure is for the *baja*.

Balear The generic name of the variety of Catalan that is spoken in the Balearics, where it is co-official with Castilian. Despite numerous differences between Balear and Central Catalan, they are generally considered to be varieties of the same language — and certainly so by linguists. On the other hand, the differences are sufficient to argue that Balear is a language in its own right, which is the stance taken by Balear nationalists. The Catalan language was taken to the Balearics by settlers from Roussillon and the Empordà during the Reconquest, and Balear still keeps certain features of the speech of those times. Especially characteristic is the use of the definite articles *es, sa, s'* and *ses*, (*el, la, l'* and *les* in Catalan and Valencian), hence place names like Ses Salines and Es Castell. (Interestingly, traces of these forms still remain in Catalonia itself, as in S'Agaró on the Costa Brava.) Within Balear there is also a great deal of dialectal variety, with distinctions made between Mallorcan *(mallorquí/mallorquín)*, Ibizan *(eivissenc/ibicenco*, including Formentera) and Minorcan *(menorquí/menorquín)*.

29

Balneario Slipped disc? Get yourself to AlbaNatura in Albacete province. If acne is your problem, you might want to zoom over to Frontera in Santa Cruz de Tenerife. And if you're suffering from neurosis (and who isn't in this day and age?) then a trip to Lanjarón in Granada is in order. A *balneario* (from *balneum*, the Latin word for bath) is a spa, and spas are now really hot. Whatever's wrong with you, somewhere in Spain there's a *balneario* which will (help to) put it right, as we discovered in amazement at www.guiasbalnearios.com where you can choose your spa by **comunidad autónoma,** province or treatment/ailment. The formal (and pompous) definition of *balneario* is "a therapeutic institution in which three basic elements converge: mineral medicinal water, appropriate installations for the correct application of the spa treatments prescribed, and a medical and ancillary team that directs the use of the methods on each patient". Beginning to sound a bit grim, right? (Our translation deliberately reflects the humourless, funless Spanish). In fact, the *balneario* is a jargon-bristling fantasy world of its own. *Algoterapia,* for example, is seaweed therapy and a *baño cleopatra* is, disappointingly, not a bath in asses milk but employs some kind of moisturiser. The *baño galvánico* (in which electric currents are applied) sounds more like a torture. *Clapping* (sic) is "a manual physiotherapy technique applied to the thorax to facilitate expectoration and mucous secretion", while the *ducha escocesa* is an alternating hot-and-cold shower applied over the whole body. The *maniluvio* is a partial bath of the hands and part of the arms, and the *pediluvio*, logically, is a foot bath. We've come a long way since the days when Valerie was dragged around Caldes de Boí (in the Catalan Pyrenees) by her psoriasis-suffering mother-in-law carrying a little glass in a special basket to drink absolutely foul sulphurous waters, and was kept awake at night by the clattering of walking sticks along the landings of the rustic wooden hotel.

Balompié Literally, ball-foot. In fact, a doomed attempt by the **Real Academia** way back in 1920 to replace the Anglicism *fútbol* with a homegrown equivalent. No-one, but no-one uses it, apart from the members and fans of the football teams Real Betis Balompié (from Sevilla) and Albacete Balompié. Handball, on the other hand (a popular sport in Spain) has always been *balonmano* (lit. ball-hand).

Bambas *Bambas*, in Catalonia at any rate, are trainers. According to the **Real Academia**, the original word is Wamba®, a registered trademark, which they define as a type of *playera* (a canvas slipper). Get real! Bambas are Nike, and Puma and Adidas... all the cool gear that football icons and tennis stars advertise on TV, so the kids absolutely have to have them, and it costs you an arm and a leg (an eye from the face, or a kidney, as the Spanish say) because they're growing so fast that you have to buy new ones every two months.... However, in Andalusia, says Theresa, they're called *tenis* (tennis shoes).

Basura, basurero. Rubbish and dustmen, or rather, refuse collectors. They do their dirty work in the middle of the night, cruising the streets in giant flashing machines from a Blade-Runner future, pulverising their pickings from bins the size of garden sheds, terrorising alley cats and drunks, and keeping insomniacs awake with their lights and clunkings and screechings.

For their dubious services you pay a periodic bill to the town hall. The amount varies, depending on where you live, and is normally combined with your water rates. In Theresa's village householders pay around 24 euros for their two-monthly water and rubbish rates, and the rural dustcarts, we're happy to say, do the rounds in the afternoon. In Barcelona, a metropolitan tax on the treatment of municipal waste is included on the quarterly water bill. How the tax is calculated is totally beyond us. For example, on one bill of Valerie's the water came to 65,80 euros and the tax was 5,10. However on another, the water was 28,01 and the tax was 9,48. Go figure.

31

Batería What makes your family of remote controls tick are *las pilas*, but what runs flat in your car when you leave the lights on all night is *la batería*, the car battery. Other *baterías* you inevitably forget to charge are those of your mobile phone and your digital camera. Completely unrelated, *aparcar en batería* is to park square, either bonnet or boot first into the kerb/gutter/ditch. Finally, *tocar la batería* is what Phil Collins does (play the drums). And, if he's down on his luck, he may be forced to bang on *una batería de cocina*, a set of saucepans.

Bikbaparoob One cold winter long ago when Theresa's understanding of Spanish did not stretch to mangled mutations of English brand names, she was terribly bunged-up and couldn't breathe. Francisco, full of a new lover's concern, tucked her up in bed and said: "What you need is 'bikbaparoob'." ¿Qué? "You know, 'bikbaparoob'?" She didn't. (A Little Richard song, perhaps? A- bik-ba-pa-roob, a-lop-bam-boom?) Minutes later her hero returned, flourishing a familiar-looking blue-and-turquoise pot. Silly her. Vick's VapoRub. The reason she hadn't understood him was because in Spanish the letters "b" and "v"(see **V** Uve) are pronounced exactly the same, like the hard "b" in Barcelona.

BOE Boletín Oficial del Estado. Bulletins are meant to be brief and to the point. Not so the BOE, published monthly with details of all government resolutions and decrees, and available at www.boe.es for those privileged few who understand Spanish legalese and have several months to spare.

Bollería The world of sweet things is complicated in Spanish. *Bollos* are bun-like cakes and include doughnuts, croissants, curranty buns, apple slices and pastries, but not fancy cakes (*pasteles*) with cream and chocolate and other gooey fillings. Not to be confused with *bulería*, a type of flamenco song and dance, (un)suitably rockified on the world's TV screens by pop star David Bisbal.

Bable   Boquerones **Bambas**   Balneario
Baja   **Basura** Bufete **Balneario** Bollycao **Boquerones** **Bolsa**
Baja   Basura

Bollycao If your kids go to school with Spanish children, sooner or later they're going to be asking for empty calories in the form of a *bollycao* – a synthetic chocolate-in-white-bread affair. However, if you look young and lovely you may find yourself being described as one. It's not a back-handed compliment, honest. It just means you're as yummy (?) as an industrially-produced chocolate bun. Other more spring-chicken-type compliments include *yogur* (yoghurt) and *petit suisse* (a make of *fromage frais*). When it's your Spanish friend's birthday and he/she moans about the advancing years, do say: *"Pero eres un bollycao/yogur/petit suisse!"* Don't say: *"Eres un cuajado (a pot of curdled milk)."*

Bolsa, bolso Generic word for any kind of bag, and handbag. We still get these mixed up. What you need from the supermarket check-out *chica* is *"una bolsa"*. Shopping bags, plastic bags, bin bags and teabags are all *bolsas* — *bolsas de la compra, bolsas de plástico, bolsas de basura, bolsas de té* and so on. What you put your make-up, money and kitchen sink in is *un bolso*. Just to muddy the waters, that important financial institution, the Stock Exchange, turns out to be nothing but a great big nondescript bag: La Bolsa.

Bono Voucher, coupon, pre-paid travel card. A shop may offer you *un bono* for returned goods. *Bonos del Tesoro* or *del Estado* are Treasury bonds. You can buy 10-ticket *bonos* for the buses and metro. Not to be confused with Irish demi-god El Bono. Or the ex-Minister of Defence, José Bono.

Bonificación The word *bono* comes from the Latin "bonus", but a bonus at work is *una bonificación* (or *un plus* or *una gratificación*). A no-claims bonus on your car insurance is succinctness itself: *bonificación por falta de siniestralidad.*

Bomberos, cuerpo de bomberos, coche de bomberos Firepersons, the fire brigade, and fire engine. Many Spaniards are convinced that the word *bomberos* is an Anglicism and will tell you how the "bom-bers" came in their "bom-bers" car to put out the fire. Tell them about firemen and fire engines and they think you're pulling their leg. What should you do, however, when you need the men in yellow to bomb over to your place? Good question. There is no child's-play-to-remember 999. Memorise 112 for emergency services, or 080 for the fire service. Or grab the Yellow Pages while your house burns down.

Boquerones Geordies, Scousers, Brummies, we're used to nicknames for people born in a particular area. How much more exciting to be named after a little fish. Those born in Malaga are either called *malagueños* or *boquerones*, unsalted anchovies. Not surprising when you consider that Malaga is famed for all kinds of fried fish in general, and *boquerones* in particular.

Botellón From *botella,* meaning literally, '"great big bottle". Aka, large, outdoor, why-pay-through-the-nose-in-a-bar-or-club alcohol fest much favoured by students, on-the-doles, low-paids, TEFL teachers and skinflints. Great when you're in it; hell if it's on your doorstep or if your car's parked anywhere nearby. Necessary ingredients: hundreds of young people looking to get drunk as cheaply as possible; one large public space, preferably in the centre of town in a residential area; scores of kiosk-type shops selling limitless supplies of litre-plus buckets of dead cheap, watered-down spirits and mixers; and a town hall that finds it has neither the authority nor the resources to prevent the resulting noise and mess. The crackdown on open-air binge drinking is, however, under way. Some autonomous communities, such as Madrid, Extremadura, The Canary Islands, and Valencia have implemented *anti-botellón* laws, and others are sure to follow suit.

Brindis A toast. When the German soldiers of Carlos V (Holy Roman Emperor, and the first Hapsburg King of Spain) sacked Rome in 1527, they went on a celebratory binge, raising their glasses and yelling "bring dir's" (literally "I offer to you"). The Italians morphed it into *"brindisi"* and from there it was a dropped syllable away from the Spanish *brindis.*

¡Venga, un brindis! Let's drink a toast! When you clink glasses in Spain you usually say "¡Salud! (Good health!)". In Catalonia, you may hear a somewhat ruder variation: *"Salut, i força al canut!* (Good health and strength to your *canuto*, er, your willy, if you have one)." Another drinking chant, which requires you to move your glass in the appropriate direction before downing the contents in one, goes like this: *"¡Arriba, abajo, al centro, p'adentro* (Up, down, in the middle, down the hatch)!"

Bufete Law practice (*bufete de abogados*). The word *bufete* may sound faintly ridiculous to some as it evokes the expressive Catalan word *"bufar"* (to puff), possibly not un-associated with the common perception of lawyers as irremediable windbags. Also, it seems to echo both the Pitufos and the Barrufets, the Castilian and Catalan versions of the Smurfs.

35

Burocracia Bureaucracy. What makes paperwork so often a task both Herculean and Kafkaesque are the following:
i. There are so many extra layers of it — the *burocracia autonómica* and the *provincial* besides the *municipal* and *estatal*.
ii. The inscrutable prose of officialdom has not budged one iota for the last several hundred years. There is no equivalent of a Plain English campaign.
iii. There are no user-friendly help leaflets explaining where you have to go and what you have to do and which documents you need.
iv. The Law of "Falta Uno". However many documents and

photocopies you take along there will always be One Missing.

Advice from those who have been there and done that on many occasions: Be patient. Be assertive. Always take ALL your papers with you whenever you go off to do something bureaucratic. Always make photocopies of everything at every stage. Take reading matter. Rope in a friendly mentor who speaks Spanish (and Catalan, where necessary). Check any papers you are given with a fine toothcomb, names, dates, account numbers, etc. BEFORE you leave the desk or **ventanilla** (window). Any undiscovered glitch may set you back years. Oh, and don't forget the rabbit's foot.

Burrocracia One of the better Spanish plays on words. *Burro* means donkey. The joke hinges on the different pronunciation of "r" and "rr", neither of which expats can pronounce properly.

Burofax This is the name of Correos' registered fax service, whereby you can send and receive faxes without having a personal fax terminal. The fax can be delivered to the recipient's physical address with recorded delivery in the manner of an urgent registered letter, and so this is the method of choice for sending exact copies of documents like summonses, cheques, claims, invoices, deeds and so on. A *burofax* with a certified copy is valid as legal proof. And now you don't even need to stand in a queue at the post office clutching your papers: assuming you have the technology, you can burofax straight from your computer and pay by credit card.

Burrofax One summer Saturday, when the kids were small, on the way out of Barcelona Valerie and husband Enric stopped at a local Oficina de **Correos** just before closing time to send a burofax (some last-minute business of Enric's). Three hours later, when they arrived at their mountain house, they heard the frenzied braying of a *burro* (donkey) echoing over the valley from a stable in the village. *"¡Qué rápido!"* said Enric. *"¡Ya ha llegado el burrofax!* (The burrofax is here!)."

Butanero Gas-bottle deliverer. In the UK the "missus" runs off with the milkman. In Spain, a chap bearing a hefty orange gas-bottle on his shoulder does the honours. Mr. Purveyor of Butane Gas Bottles and his truck do the rounds daily but will only visit your apartment block/street/outlying hamlet on specified days. You either call to place your order with one of the two main gas providers, Repsol Butano or Cepsa, or stick your neck out of the window and yell: *"Butanero, número siete."* Just don't forget to tip the chap towards his osteopath fees. Alternatively, you can drive down to a distribution depot and do your own back in. Until 2002 Repsol had a monopoly on distribution, then Cepsa broke the orange mould and brought out lighter, silver-coloured bottles.

Before acquiring your own personal *bombona* (the gas-bottle itself), you must fill out and sign a contract. Happily, running out of gas at night or after midday on Saturday no longer means knocking on your neighbour's door to borrow a 10-ton equivalent of a bowl of sugar: in these enlightened times you can avoid grovelling and seeming hugely unorganised by popping down to your local *gasolinera* (petrol station), some of which are now allowed to sell the back-breaking bottles.

C

Cabildo insular Island Council, a local government corporation specific to the Canary Islands. Each of the seven islands is administered by its *cabildo*.

Café Coffee, or a place serving drinks. Ordering coffee the way you like it is one of the first things you learn in Spanish. Learning to order what everyone else in your group wants will take you rather longer. Especially if you're in Malaga, where you can ask for *una nube* (a cloud: i.e. lots of milk not much coffee), *un sombra* (a shadow: more coffee than in a *nube*) and *un mitad* (half-coffee, half-milk). For some reason, a large cup of watered-down black coffee is *un café americano,* and a short strong coffee with a dash of milk is *un cortado*. Thankfully, outside the major capitals the High Street has not yet been invaded by Starbucks. Excellent, unpretentious coffee is to be found in every street-corner bar — and it's still served in cups or glasses. Not super-sized buckets holding enough milk to liquidate the lactose-intolerant.

Caja de ahorros The savings bank also belongs under the **entidad bancaria** umbrella. The *cajas*, most of which are regionally based, provide the same services (and lousy interest rates) as banks. However they do not have shareholders, but are legally constituted as non-profit foundations and return a large part of their profits to society via their *obra social* (social, educational, scientific and cultural projects, or community welfare as the Fundación Caja Madrid website nicely translates it) and still manage to be richer than banks. La Caixa Foundation, for example, besides owning the Cosmocaixa science museums in Madrid and Barcelona, funds a host of

39

initiatives from Alzheimer research to postgrad scholarships to local libraries. And it was the Fundació Caixa Catalunya that bought, restored and now manages Gaudí's World Heritage building, La Pedrera.

Caló The dialect spoken by Spain's 650,000-strong **gitano** (gypsy) community. The word *caló* itself means "dark" and the word for *gitano* in *caló* is *calé,* meaning "the dark ones." In the encyclopaedia *Ethnologue: Languages of the World* (15th edition, editor Gordon, Raymond G., Jr. Dallas, Texas: SIL International), *caló* is classified as one of the 13 living languages of Spain. Described as a blend of native Romany vocabulary and Spanish grammar, many *caló* words and expressions have entered colloquial Spanish through flamenco lyrics, **andaluz** and criminal jargon. When we were still struggling with standard school-book Spanish, these were the kinds of words we never understood in pop songs, films and rapid-fire conversation among streetwise friends. While we gradually incorporated some of the expressions into our vocabulary, it was only during the research for this entry that we realised how many came from the language of the *gitanos*. Some common *caló* words are *chachi* (good, cute, neat), *currar* (*trabajar* - to work), *largarse* (*irse* - to go, clear off, split), *el trullo* (*la carcel* – prison/the nick), *mangar* (*robar* – to steal, nick), *bufetear* (to have breakfast) and the fabulous *motoro* (a motorised police officer).

Caló has not only enriched Castilian Spanish but also **catalán**, **vasco** and **gallego** through the regional variations *catalán-caló, vasco-caló* and *gallego-luso-caló*. Variations of *caló* are also spoken in Portugal, Brazil and France. Interestingly, in Latin America, *caló* refers to a variety of Spanish mixed with Mexican underworld slang and a great many English words.

Callista Chiropodist. *Callista* is the colloquial term, although some *callistas* themselves understandably prefer to be known as *podólogos* (and now, moreover, they have upgraded themselves to *podiatristas*.) However be careful: a *podólogo* may also be a qualified doctor who specialises in foot surgery and will not be pleased at having his/her time wasted with your corns and calluses. In her early days here, Valerie made an appointment with a *podólogo* for what turned out to be a massive outbreak of verrucas. She was swiftly ejected from the **consulta** with barely disguised distaste. Did she not have any bunions, any truly spectacular malformations to get a scalpel into? By the way, don't be offended if your *callista* wears a mask.

Caminos Have you ever been puzzled to meet or hear of someone who's studying *caminos* (literally ways)? This is short for Caminos, Canales y Puertos: i.e. civil engineering. A civil engineer is *un ingeniero de caminos, canales y puertos*.

Camino de Santiago Years ago we read an article about A Man Who Had It All, an accounts executive at a big ad agency in Madrid, who threw it all away to run a refuge on one of the most desolate, isolated mountain passes on the Camino de Santiago, known in English as the Way of St James, and in **gallego** as the Ruta Xacobea.

Promoting the Way helps boost tourism to relatively underdeveloped **Galicia** , but it is still serious stuff for the spiritual seeker. Since medieval times, Santiago de Compostela has ranked alongside Rome and Jerusalem as one of the most important Christian pilgrimage destinations, and now attracts a growing number of modern pilgrims from around the globe. They hike or bike, and ride horses or donkeys from starting points across Europe for weeks or months to visit the cathedral in Santiago where, legend has it, the mortal remains of the apostle Saint James the Great were discovered, having been carried to northern Spain by boat from Jerusalem.

You may be wondering what exactly the connection is between Santiago and St James, and also with the word Xacobeo. Or rather, if Santiago and St James were the same person, why the different names? Think of it as Sant-iago. Iago is the Spanish version of the Latin name Jacobus. Parallel to this, in Vulgar Latin Jacobus morphed into Jacomus and then James/Jaime (and Catalan Jaume). Jacques is the French version of Jacobus, and in French scallops are called Coquilles de St Jacques, from the custom of bringing back scallop shells from Galicia as proof of having done the Camino.

In fact there are a number of Ways, linking up routes from all over Europe. The French Route is historically the most traditional of the Pilgrims' Ways and the most widely used internationally. The route, both in Spain and France, has been declared a UNESCO World Heritage Site.

Carajillo Winter-warming black coffee with liquor and sugar. A sort of no-nonsense Irish Coffee without the cream and an essential part of every self-respecting workman's breakfast. Typical *carajillo* liquors are brandy, rum or anisette. Pronounced ca-ra-HHEE-yo.

Carnaval In Theresa's carnival-going days, when she still joined in every fair and fiesta within an 90km radius, she dressed up as a scarecrow, nun, male cat and rubbish bin — first parading around town to the cheering crowds, but then, as the evening wore on, her rather pathetic, home-made outfits degenerated into dishevelled messes. Children and those looking for any excuse to party love *carnaval.* Held in the week leading up to Ash Wednesday (some time in February), every town and village organises fancy-dress parades and street celebrations. On mainland Spain, it is Cádiz where the most spectacular carnival takes place, and where the most fun is to be had. For 10 days (or rather, nights), groups of *gaditanos* (natives of Cádiz) dress up in jazzy costumes, and line up on elaborate stages or converge on street corners to sing and chant *chirrigotas*, humorous verses that are clever, witty, rude, crude, cruel, absurd and always topical, poking fun at politicians and celebrities and reviewing the year's events.

But even the Cádiz carnival pales in splendour and party-till-you-dropness beside the one held in Santa Cruz, capital of Tenerife. Rivalled only by Río, the Canary Islanders party for a whole three weeks. There are beauty pageants, horse parades, masked parades, vintage car cavalcades, top Latino groups playing in the streets, opera, competitions of street bands etc. Most famous of all, attracting visitors from all over the world, is the Drag Queen pageant, during which, it seems, the entire city cross dresses for the night. For a number of years after the Civil War, Franco banned carnival, but the citizens of Santa Cruz just changed the name to "Winter Festival" and carried on partying. Wearing their disguises and masks, the revellers were often chased through the streets by the police. One year, apparently so many people were arrested that they were herded into the bullring because the local prison was full.

Carnet de conducir A Spanish driver's licence must be renewed every 10 years. Once you get to 45, you must have a check-up (*revisión médica*) every five years until the age of 70, and after that, every two years. Mostly to make sure you can still see. Rigorous it is not. In less than five minutes Theresa saw three "doctors". The first one had her read a chart of letters. The second smoked a cigarette while she attempted to keep a ball between two moving lines on a prehistoric computer screen. The third asked her if she had any illnesses or addictions. She said "No". They all signed a piece of paper and she handed over €35.

Carrera Your *carrera profesional* is your career, your *carrera universitaria* is your degree or university course, and *carrera* also means race in all its meanings. It also means a ladder in stockings or tights. Congested city streets are *una carrera de obstáculos* and *las carreras* are the races.

Carta certificada Registered letter. If it doesn't arrive, you have to hang on for a nail-biting 30 days before they will trace it. Theresa waited six months for compensation for a packet of lost colour slides — and was awarded the princely sum of 30 euros.

44

Castellano Castilian Spanish. See **español**. Today *castellano* is used to refer to the Spanish spoken in Spain, a respectful term to distinguish it from the co-official Galician, Catalan and Basque, and also Asturian, Aragonese, Aranese and one or two other minority languages, all of which are, logically, Spanish in that they are native to Spain. In fact, Castilian was originally just another dialect of the Latin spoken in Hispania. It originated in Castile in the eighth century and, depending on where you're from and how you look at it, was imposed on/spread through the rest of the Peninsula in later centuries, and then through the New World. The Spanish constitution calls it *castellano* but the institution that regulates it is called the **Real Academia Española**.

Catalán For the unprepared, the Catalan language (not "dialect" — the one gaffe you must never ever make, unless you want to get up a Catalan's nose big time) can come as a bit of a shock because it sounds quite different from Spanish: short, sharp — and nasty, anti-Catalans are hasty to add. Valerie's late Catalan father-in-law once told an anecdote, in his usual deadpan way, that had the whole family rolling on the floor with laughter. During the Franco days, he was travelling from Barcelona to Madrid by train with a friend on business. Naturally, the two men conversed in Catalan. In the same compartment was a Madrid lady with a lapdog. As the train chugged into Madrid, the dog began to bark in a frenzy of excitement. "But of course!" said the lady. "He has heard barking, and he has replied."

On paper, Catalan looks rather more familiar, like a cross between Spanish, French and Italian. It isn't a hybrid at all, though, but a descendant in its own right of the Latin spoken in the northern Iberian peninsula during the Roman empire, and thus a sister language of Spanish, French, Italian, Portuguese, Provençal and Romanian. The Spanish Constitution of 1978 lays down that in Catalonia and the Balearic Islands, *el català* is co-official with **castellano**. It is spoken by more than six million people and understood by almost 10 million (which is more than some of the official languages of the EU) in Catalonia, the Community of Valencia (where it is called **valencià**), the Balearic Islands, Roussillon in southern France, Andorra, the Franja de Ponent (a strip of Aragon bordering on Catalonia), El Carche (a small area of Murcia), and Alghero in Sardinia (where it is co-official with Italian and Sardinian). Catalan covers a very wide continuum of dialects and is sometimes referred to as *català-valencià-balear*. The Catalan literary tradition dates from the 12th century and boasts its very own blockbuster, *Tirant lo Blanc*, a novel of chivalry written in Valencia by Joanot Martorell in the second half of the 15th century. Highly praised

45

by Cervantes and regarded by some critics as the best European novel of the 15th century, *Tirant* is now a major motion picture directed by Vicente Aranda.

Catalunya The Catalan name for Catalonia, Cataluña in Castilian. Valerie once received hate mail (okay, one email) from a Catalan fanatic, written in utterly bizarre Catalanglish. His complaint? In an article of hers about the Catalans posted at her then website, the name Cataluña was used (an editor had changed it from Catalunya.) This nut told Valerie she had mortally offended his country, because "Cataluña" didn't exist. Fortunately, most Catalans are not so confused about the way you spell a place name and the place itself. The real hornet's nest issue is whether Catalonia/Catalunya/Cataluña is a country, a region, a nation, a nationality, or an ethnic group — or how you define these terms. During the recent row about the new statute for the region, a Costa Blanca paper's front page trumpeted: "Valencia is not Catalonia." Quite.

Catastro Although the first association that springs to mind is catastrophe, in fact the Catastro is the Land Registry (from the Greek term *katastichon* meaning register - literally line by line) and the *valor catastral* of your property is the registered value of the land. This is the place you go when your neighbour hammers at your door three weeks after you have moved into your charming rustic property and claims that the bit sticking out at the bottom of the plot where you've got your water tank is his. Every *escritura* (title deed) has a Catastro number on it, for which the Land Registry holds a corresponding plan. They hold the original but will let you have a photocopy. So clutching what you hope is proof of ownership of the disputed three square metres, you take the plan home, pore over it with a magnifying glass, and realise that while the water deposit plot is, in fact, yours, the ground level wood store and half of the garden seem to be classified as common land. You wave the plan at the would-be usurper, who protests too much (victory is yours), and then stash the document at the bottom of a dusty file and pray that no-one ever tries to reclaim the pavement.

Catering (pronounced 'catterin') or *cáterin* as the **Real Academia** suggests, in addition to referring to the business of providing meals, has also come to mean the premises or shop where the food is made/sold – a place where you can buy ready-made meals.

Cementerio The Spanish add a whole new dimension to the meaning of bury (put in a hole and cover). When you die, in many cemeteries you are "buried" above ground, in one of hundreds of niches set in a multi-storey wall. The penthouse niches and the ones two inches from the ground are the cheapest as tending them requires either risking life and limb up a municipal ladder or scrabbling around on your hands and knees on the concrete. Life on the other side may last all eternity, but your earthly resting place will probably be somewhat briefer. Due to lack of space, especially in urban cemeteries, most niches are rented not sold and, depending on the municipality, you may find yourself out on what's left of your ear only a few years after your burial. After that time, your relations must renew the lease, or dispose of your remains as they see fit, or else let you join everyone else who's been turfed out into a common grave. Not surprisingly, cremation is on the increase. Once frowned upon by the Catholic Church, the practice is now widely accepted, and cremations account for about 20 per cent of the market.

Cena, cenar Dinner, and to have dinner. Contrary to all medical advice everywhere, rarely eaten before 10pm. The only people in a restaurant before this time are the waiters — and the *guiris*.

Cercanías Environs, surrounding area, as in *Madrid y sus cercanías*. Un *tren de cercanías* is a local or suburban train. **Renfe**'s Cercanías service is province-wide.

Ch The 4th letter of the Spanish alphabet, called "che", as in Che Guevara.

Chacha Short for *muchacha*, girl, lass, wench. Used to refer to the domestic help: *la chacha*. See **asistenta**.

Chapuza Botched job. Obviously, very common word. Also used to refer to a job well done that someone else did. It seems to be a Pavlovian reflex for any kind of workman to ask, indignantly: "¿Pero quién te hizo esta chapuza (who is responsible for this seriously sub-standard piece of shoddiness)?" when he sees someone else's work, even if (or possibly because) it's well done. The person who does a *chapuza* is a *chapucero*.

48

Chaval, chavala Colloquial word for boy or girl, rather like lad and lass. Carries no negative connotations whatsoever and thus has nothing to do with the English "chav". Or does it? *Chaval* is of gypsy origin and comes from the **caló** for "boy" (*chavo*) or "son" (*chavi*). While the origin of the English "chav" is disputed, both the Collins English Dictionary and the Oxford Advanced Learners' Dictionary advance the Romany *chavo/chavi* derivation/distortion. We prefer the politically incorrect backronym "Council Housed And Violent".

Chiringuito Conjures up images of sunny Sunday lunchtimes spent tucking into buckets of *pescadito frito* (fried fish), sardines on sticks, juicy fat prawns and *tinto de verano* (red wine and lemonade). Strictly speaking, a wooden shack serving drinks and basic snacks, but more often than not refers to a fish restaurant, basic or otherwise, on the sea front.

Chorizo The famous spicy sausage is inextricably linked in our minds with the petty thief, small time crook or yob, which has spawned the verb *chorizar*, to swipe, nick, pinch. What has a spicy sausage got to do with pinching someone else's gear? Nothing, according to our research: the second meaning of *chorizo* originates from the gypsy word *chori*, a petty thief, but seems to have been influenced by the existing *chorizo* and finally assimilated by it. *Chorizo,* the sausage, is made of pork and cured using Spanish paprika, which gives a deep red color and rich smoky flavor. In fact there is a bewildering array of different *chorizos*: long thin ones *(chistorra)*, those flavoured with spicy paprika or sweet paprika, mini cocktail ones *(choricitos),* fat coarse ground ones *(cantimpalo)*...

Chucherías (chuches) Teeth-rotting lollipops and rubbery worms and horrible pink squashy things and sickly objects in funny shapes and lurid colours, and all the stuff that children whine for and fight over and are given in bags after parties. And are gorged on by all ages.

49

Chuleta Ostensibly a chop, pork or lamb, but also a crib sheet and an essential part of any self-respecting school kid's armoury. There is no stigma attached to cheating in exams. On the contrary, the inventors of particularly ingenious *chuletas* are much admired by their peers.

Chulo Awesome/cool/cute/wicked or any "nice" equivalent currently in vogue, as in your new dress *"es muy chulo* (really cool)". You can also *ponerse chulo* (lit. put yourself *chulo),* meaning to act impertinently or get stroppy. Then there's *chulo* the noun, used to refer to those who swagger through life with puffed-up pride. Think Delboy. Finally, a *chulo* is someone who lives off a prostitute's earnings. In other words, a pimp.

Chungo When Valerie's about-to-retire dentist announced that one of her teeth was *chungo*, she knew this teenage slang word had finally been absorbed into the mainstream. *Chungo* means bad, ill, tough, difficult, rotten, unpleasant, malfunctioning and all those things and more. In a word: dodgy.

Chupa Chups In the mid-1950s, when Spain was a languishing backwater under Franco's dictatorship, a sweet manufacturer in Asturias called Enric Bernat had a brilliant idea that was to change the face of sweet eating for ever. In those days, candy came in large chunks which kids would push in and out of their mouths, getting sticky hands and in general making a mess. Bernat hit on putting a kid's-mouth-sized chunk on the end of a wooden stick. And never looked back. Since the first Chupa Chup was made in 1958, his firm has grown into a world lollipop empire with industrial plants in Spain, France, Russia, China and Mexico, a whole range of candy products, and whopping sales in 170 countries. Sticks are now plastic, and flavours have increased from the original seven (boring old strawberry, lemon, mint, etc.) to 40, including cappuccino, jasmine tea and sugar-free watermelon. The daisy logo, by the way, was designed by Salvador Dalí. Oh, and Chupa Chups was the first lollipop in space, consumed by Russian cosmonauts on the Mir spaceship in 1995.

Chupito *Chupar* means to suck, slurp, lick or guzzle. A *chupito* is a measure of liquor served in an inch-high glass to be slurped down in one gulp. The Spanish are hugely fond of diminutives, adding to words suffixes like -ito –cito, –itito and –ete, which refer to something small and/or cute. A *chupete*, for example, is a baby's dummy. While it's doubtful if a *chupito* of tequila can be considered cute, the word itself somehow makes it sound less of a serious drink. Restaurants are fond of inviting you to a *chupito* of their very worst liquors to thank you for your custom. Watch out for sickly banana concoctions, anything paraffin-blue, and *aguardiente* (firewater).

Churros Years ago, when Valerie smoked like a chimney, she lost her sweet tooth, and was regarded as deeply disturbed because she preferred to put salt on her *churros* instead of sugar. *Churros* are fritters made from dough and extruded from a large piping bag into hot oil, where they are fried to a crispy texture, then dusted with sugar and (optionally) cinnamon. The best way to ingest an entire week's calorie intake in one sitting is to breakfast on a pile of them dunked in a cup of hot chocolate as thick as trifle custard. *Chocolate con churros* is also the carbohydrate fix of choice for **meriendas** and kids' parties. No festival or **feria** would be complete without the smell of frying *churros,* the roadside stalls and street vendors selling them in large paper cones, and the ravenous scoffing itself. But there are *churros* and *churros.* There are the smaller crinkly ones called *madrileños,* which some people prefer to the thicker tubular variety, known as *porras* (truncheons!) or *tejeringos* (meaning literally "I-inject-you's", from *te* + the verb to inject, *jeringar*). And just to confuse things, in Seville they are called *calentitos* (little hotties).

51

Every town has its *churrería.* Valerie has one round the corner on one of central Barcelona's busiest streets, wedged between a shop selling air-conditioners and a bar. It also sells chocolate-coated *churros,* and other fried doughnut things, and loads of different kinds of crisps, and cod fritters...and...we're getting really hungry now. You can even buy deep-frozen *churros* ready for frying. And no doubt someone has invented microwave *churros,* even more of an aberration than the microwave chips consumed by Valerie's mother in Manchester.

Churri Slang for girl, girlfriend, with connotations of babies, cute things. Have been unable to find out where this originates from, but could be **caló,** the language of Spain's gypsies.

CIF Código Identificación Fiscal — the corporate tax identification number required by all limited companies, co-operatives or other larger-than-one-person businesses. Definitely to be confused with NIF, Número de Identificación Fiscal (an individual's tax identification number) or NIE, Número de Identificación de Extranjero (bloody foreigner's number). You cannot do anything legal or fiscal without having your own NIE, which is also your NIF. So that's cleared that up then. But definitely not to be confused with Cif, a creamy-white bathroom cleaning fluid known in English as JIF, which left unchanged would have been an unmarketable "Gghhif".

Coco Coconut, brains ("nut") and bogeyman. Admittedly "Rock-a-bye baby" doesn't end too happily for baby, but the Spanish version, sung to the same tune (Johannes Brahms' *Wiegenlied*), is positively terrifying. *"Duérmete niño, duérmete ya, que viene el coco, y te llevará/comerá."* Translation: "Sleep little child, I mean sleep NOW, or the *coco* (dreaded ghost-like monster with a three-holed head like a coconut) will snatch you away/gobble you up."

Cofradía Religious brotherhood whose members dress up in sinister pointy-hats, masks and floor-length robes at Easter to mourn the death/celebrate the resurrection of Jesus Christ. The most privileged members, however, don black suits and ties, and inflict wounds on themeselves by bearing 10-ton Jesus and Mary thrones on their shoulders through the streets for 12 hours at a time. No food, no drink (apart from water), no rest. To make the task even more gruelling, the truly repentant bear their burden blindfolded.

Cojones/cojines/cajones *Cojones* are "balls" (testicles) but the word is not used to mean "balls" as in a load of old bollocks). It's a colloquial (okay, vulgar) interjection used, as the **Real Academia** delicately puts it, to express diverse mood states, especially surprise or anger. This hardly begins to do it justice. *¡Qué cojones!* What the hell! What a bloody cheek!

Cojones are the body part of choice for most visceral reactions: if you are *hasta los cojones,* you are fed up/pissed off. If you have *cojones* (one of the highest accolades you can get, in fact), you have guts. If you say what comes out of your *cojones*, you say what you bloody well feel like. If you are touching your (own) *cojones,* you're sitting around on your butt doing bugger all, and if you're touching someone else's, you're getting up their nose. And you can do all these things even if you're a woman! Though it has to be said you will hear some women striking a claim for body-part equality by replacing *cojones* with *ovarios,* as in *estoy hasta los ovarios,* don't touch my *ovarios,* and so on.

However, *cojones* are probably doomed forever to be muddled by foreigners with *cojines* (cushions) and *cajones* (drawers). There isn't a native English speaker of Spanish in the world who doesn't have an embarrassing *cajón/cojín/cojón* tale to tell. Theresa's involved instructing a class of 11-year olds to stuff large *cojones* up their jumpers as part of a costume for a Christmas play. Years later, they would still say: "Do you remember, *Seño* (Miss), *cuando*...?"

So, if your surname is Jones (and most especially if your initials are C.O.), you have been warned.

Cojonudo If someone or something is *cojonudo*, they rock. Literally, this slang word means "endowed with balls", but now it is equally applied to anyone and anything, and means great, brilliant, etc. The current edition of the *Diccionario de la Real Academia* labels it "vulgar" but tells us that in the next edition it will be slightly softened to "colloquial and sounding a bit off".

Colega Colleague, in theory. But not really. More like mate or buddy for the under-25s, an acquaintance, rather than a big *amigo*. At a business meeting, rather than saying: "This is my *colega*, Juan/Juanita," try: "This is my *compañero de trabajo*." Can also be used as in a watch-it-matey sort of a way, as in: "Oye, colega".

Comarca Sometimes translated as "county", the *comarca* is a geographical subdivision of a province. In **Catalonia** and Aragon, the *comarca* is also a local administrative district with its own council (*consejo/consell comarcal*).

Comedor Dining room, in a house, workplace or school. Also used to mean school dinners or the act of staying at school for lunch, as in "*Tengo mi Joselito en comedor* (My little José stays for school dinners)". At state schools, which finish at 2pm, *comedor* lasts until around 4pm and serves as an essential babysitting service for busy parents (timetables may vary in some autonomous communities). Private schools tend to have school in the morning and afternoon, and the lunch hour will be staggered from around 1pm onwards. Like our once-upon-a-time stodgy but healthful school dinners, in Spain they are nutritious, filling and sometimes despised. Lots of vegetables, fish, pulses, lentils, soups, meat, rice, pasta, and finished off with fruit or yoghurt.

Comida Lunch. Eating is serious business in Spain. It is not rocket and smoked salmon on rye, designer sushi, a macrobiotic soya-burger or a slice of quiche grabbed in a half-hour break. True, your average teenager would probably rather have *una hamburguesa* en *El Burger*, but many people still tuck into a hearty lunch at Spanish midday (2.30–3pm). Those that can't make it home go for a three-course menu in family-run restaurants packed out with labourers, businessmen, and thrifty tourists overjoyed to be getting all that grub for around seven euros.

El menú goes something like this: huge plate of homemade soup, beany-type potage or *espagetis*; a main course of meat or fish and salad or fries; and then rice pudding, custard, creme caramel, ice-cream or fruit. Bread, beer, wine or a soft drink is usually included and if you go for "workman's choice", *vino con gaseosa* (thick red plonk and lemonade), the bottle's yours. Usually finished off with a coffee and perhaps a glass of cognac or anisette to settle the stomach. And so to work.

Comisaría Police Station, and a relic of the police state that Spain once was. Where you go to report a crime, and also where nationals apply for their I.D. cards and passports. It is also the place where you apply for or renew your residence permit. A relatively painless affair these days — we remember the time when you could look forward to a thrilling morning or two huddled in an endless, smoke-filled queue, quite convinced you were a mass murderer. Almost unbelievably, passports are now processed on the same day. Your residence permit, on the other hand, may have expired by the time it comes through.

55

The head of a *comisaría* (co-mi-sa-REE-a) is a *comisario* (co-mi-SA-ree-o) or *comisaria*, a word also used to describe someone in charge of organising a event such as an exhibition, a sports race or a trade fair.

Comunidad Autónoma A self-governing region. Spain is divided into 17 *comunidades autónomas*. Ten of the communities are composed of several **provincias**, the other seven of just one (Asturias, Baleares, Cantabria, La Rioja, **Madrid**, Murcia and Navarra). The constitution of 1978 established the right to self-government of Spain's regions and "historical nationalities", an attempt at a neutral term which was coined to refer to Catalonia, the Basque Country, and **Galicia**, while sidestepping the issue of whether they are nations or peoples (still a tough issue, as recent ructions about the Catalans' bid to modify their Statue of Autonomy have shown). It also put in place a process whereby individual provinces, or groups of provinces with common historical, cultural and economic characteristics, the island territories, and provinces with a regional historical identity could accede to self-government and become autonomous communities. They were implemented by statute, and created by stages from 1979 to 1983.

Comunidad de propietarios Owners' association. When you buy your urban-dream penthouse or bijou apartment, congrats: you are now an owner of a *propiedad horizontal* (joint freehold, US condo) and, besides paying your share of joint costs, will attend assemblies where mind-numbing rants about blocked drainpipes, cockroach infestations, communal satellite dishes and crumbling facades ignite the basest passions.

Consell insular Catalan-Balear for Island Council. A local government body midway between the *municipios* and the autonomous government of Baleares. There are three island councils: one for Mallorca, one for Menorca, and one for the Pitiusas (Ibiza and Formentera).

Conserje Caretaker. If you live in a block of flats or an *urbanización* the *conserje* will become an important and tippable person in your life. He or she is responsible for the maintenance and cleaning of the building and communal areas but often stars in a number of other roles. During Theresa's five-year residence in a 60-square-metre rabbit hutch overlooking a communal swimming-pool, her *conserje*: received deliveries of large household appliances on her behalf, fed the cats while she was on holiday, fixed her water heater, changed a fuse or two, drove her to **Urgencias**, sold her losing tickets in the Christmas Lottery, and on more than one occasion climbed up a dodgy extending ladder to her balcony after she'd locked herself out. Well worth a couple of bottles of good Rioja at Christmas.

Carrera   Chupa chups   Caminos
Chorizo   Cenar   Carnaval   Callista   Castellano   Carnaval
       Churinguito   Comida   Chorizo   Copa

Consulta Doctor's surgery (office in American English). It refers to both the premises and the surgery hours. It can be a medical or similar practice (dentists etc.). *La consulta* is the surgery or consulting room itself, the collective practice, and the activity, e.g. *el doctor sólo tiene consulta los martes* (the doctor only has surgery on Tuesdays).

Consumición mínima A cover charge in a nightclub: literally, minimum consumption.

Convocatoria A difficult word to get the hang of. From *convocar*, meaning to announce, call or summons, as in a meeting, conference, competition, strike, exam etc. In practice also used to refer to the holding of the event announced. For example, you may read of a *convocatoria* (i.e. an announcement) for a series of new government jobs in July. If interested, you would then compete for one of the jobs in the "*convocatoria de julio*". Likewise, if you fail, say a university exam in June, there will almost certainly be another *convocatoria* (sitting) in September (and December, and January, and April etc., until you eventually pass or drop out).

Copa Either a wine glass or an alcoholic drink, but definitely not a cup, which is *una taza*. So, in a bar you ask for "*una copa de vino*" (a glass of wine) or you say to your Spanish friends: "*Vamos de copas*," Let's go out for a (few) drinks. Then, of course, you have "*una copa de más*" (one too many) and end up, as Shakespeare would have it, "in your cups".

Correos Spain's snail mail. What can we say? In the old days, the Spanish Post Office inspired total dread, like most official institutions: dark brown cavernous offices where you shuffled for hours in the wrong queue, and when it was your turn they shut the **ventanilla** in your face. All that is now relegated, we imagine, to the Museo Postal y Telegráfico in Madrid which "offers the visitor a magical and fascinating journey through the evolution of the communications media that have had a decisive influence on the development of civilisation". These days many post offices — at least in the big cities — are all quiet and digital, full of electronic number machines and bells and whistles. While you still have to physically go to the *oficina de correos* to pick up and send parcels etc., you can now do lots of stuff (for example a **burofax**) straight from your computer and pay by credit card.

So we thought about writing about how much we like the logo, the bright yellow and blue, and how now the cheerful yellow letter boxes stand out (they used to be metallic grey). You take a quick look at the logo and you can see it's a crown, a royal mail kind of thing. But what's that under the crown? A teapot? A SNAIL. We were utterly taken with the logo designer's witty reference until a friend put us right: it's a boring old post horn.

58

Corte Inglés El Corte Inglés, with its distinctive green-and-white logo, is to Spain as Selfridges is to London and Macy's to New York. But what's with the "Inglés"? Is the store full of Crabtree and Evelyn soaps, Olde English marmalade and Paddington Bears? Was it founded by an English gent? Or styled on one of London's department stores? We thought it had something to do with the royal family — after all, doesn't the shop's name translate as "The English Court"? Not even close. For a start, "The English Court" would be "La Corte", not "El Corte". "El Corte Inglés" actually translates as "The English Cut", and it takes its name from a children's tailor's founded in Madrid in 1890, a time when the Savile Row tailors of London were kings of the cloth. In 1934, a certain Mr. Ramón Areces Rodríguez bought the shop, turning it into the country's first department store in the 1950s, and setting up more branches in Spain's major cities in the 1960s.

Until the shopping mall boom in the 1990s, shops in Spain were mostly small, specialist and scattered, which helps explain the store's great success and popularity. Whatever you need — cut crystal, a Burberry jacket, silver dip, star anise, or state-of-the-art iPod — El Corte Inglés has it. Even those who complain about the prices and the airs and graces of the sales staff will admit that when you can't get a coveted item anywhere else, it's the only place to go. It is also the easiest place to buy goods on credit. In other large stores, you need to show a *nómina* or payslip, but in El Corte Inglés they only need your **NIE** or passport number and the number of your Spanish bank account.

Cuba Libre or Cubalibre Who knows what a free Cuba has to do with rum and coke. But if Bacardi and Coke is what you want, that's what you ask for. Believe us, it's easier than elongating your mouth to wide-mouthed frog proportions and asking for a Ba-CAR-dee con co-ca-CO-la..

Cubata Proper stiff drink in a long glass with a mixer. The Spanish drink their G&Ts, vodkas and tonics and whisky-Seven-Ups after dinner, not before. Hardly surprising considering the amount of *yin, bodka* and **güisqui** that goes in them. To make a Spanish *cubata*, put three or four fat ice-cubes in a long glass, pour in liquor of choice until there's just enough room to add half a bottle of Coke/Seven-Up etc. Save other half for next drink. Get a taxi home.

Cubierto It took us ages to realise, consciously, that in a restaurant, *un cubierto* is not the equivalent of a cover charge. *Un cubierto* is a place setting, comprising a plate, knife, fork, spoon, napkin and bread. By extension, it is a meal for one, at a set price: for example, *un cubierto especial*; *un cubierto de 10 euros. Los cubiertos* means the cutlery. A bit odd, perhaps, but very useful when you can't get your tongue around *cuchillos,* *tenedores y cucharas*, or even remember which is which (knives, forks and spoons, respectively).

Cuenta *"La cuenta, por favor"* is what you ask for in a restaurant when you want the bill. *Una cuenta* is also an account, a bank account, commercial account, email account. Not to be confused with *cuento*, a story or tale in all senses, including gossip. The non-politically correct *cuentos chinos* (Chinese stories) is best translated as a load of baloney; *cuentos de viejas* are old wives' tales.

Cuernos Horns. Randy ones. The phrase "to cuckold someone" fell into disuse centuries ago in English, but the Spanish equivalent, *poner los cuernos a alguien* (lit. to put the horns on someone) is very much alive and thrusting. As is the horn gesture, made with the index finger and little finger, to suggest that your partner is cheating on you, or may be about to do so. If you are looking for a choice expression to capture the verbal impact of a "Like hell!" with an angry up-yours finger, try *"¡Y un cuerno!"*

60

Defensor del Pueblo Defender of the People rolls off the tongue more easily and sounds more dynamic than ombudsman. Each autonomous community has one and there is also a supreme *Defensor* of the entire nation. Complaints about any aspect of the public administration may be presented in English online, by fax, phone or in person. The corresponding web page — unusual for a government department — is easy to understand, easy to navigate, and comes in English and French: www.defensordelpueblo.es

Delegación A regional or local office of a bank, business or government department. The Delegación de Hacienda is your local tax office, which is quite logical: it's a regional delegation of the central government. *El delegado* is the regional or area director, or the manager of a branch office of a savings bank. *Delegado* is often used where we would say representative.

Denominación de Origen (DO) For wines, this is the Spanish equivalent of the Appellation Controlée. As of 2006, there are 65 Spanish DOs, including Jerez (sherry), which is produced in and near the city of Jerez de la Frontera, in the province of Cádiz, and *cava* (meaning cellar), a sparkling wine made by the *champenoise* method mainly in the Penedès area in Catalonia. The special DOCa (Denominación de Origen Calificada) was introduced in 1991. For many years only Rioja held this lofty status, to be joined in 2001 by the marvellous Priorat, a sophisticated and sought-after red wine from the **comarca** of the same name in southern Catalonia.

61

Denominación de Origen Protegida (DOP) **What do saffron from La Mancha, hazelnuts from Reus, rice from Valencia and Teruel ham have in common?** Redolent of the magical caché of the finest of wines, the term Denominación de Origen is often used loosely to refer to any product whose quality, identity and reputation are indissolubly and exclusively linked to the place where it is produced or elaborated, like Roquefort cheese, Puy lentils and Parma ham. In fact, as far as foodstuffs are concerned, the Denominación de Origen Protegida, to give it its full official name, is a strictly regulated subcategory of the **Indicación Geográfica Protegida**, the system set up by the EU in 1992 to protect genuine products against abuse and imitation. For DOP products, all stages of production and elaboration must take place in the area in question. Spanish ones include Mahón cheese, Siurana olive oil, Asturian cider (*sidra*), Granada honey and Murcian paprika: look for the distinctive blue-and-yellow EU seal of approval.

62

Denunciar Once you have learnt the meaning of this word, chances are you won't bother with the long-winded English equivalent. *Denunciar* is to report a crime or to report someone to the authorities for doing something wrong. "*Te voy a denunciar* (I'm going to report you to the police)." Or: "*Te voy a poner una denuncia* (I'm going to make a formal complaint about you to the police)." Ah, but which police? You choose: the Policía Municipal, the Policía Nacional, the Policía Autonómica, or the **Guardia Civil.**

Whichever you decide, we hope you have more luck than Theresa did when she had her purse pinched in down-town Barcelona (while visiting Valerie), and had the even greater misfortune to make a *denuncia* at the police station in Castelldefels, the nearby town where she and Francisco were staying. It was February. Freezing cold. The building looked like something out of Dickens: all slimy drains, iron railings, brutal

brickwork and doorways built for the vertically-challenged. She and Francisco saw a few glum-looking souls standing outside. Where was the waiting room? There wasn't one. This was it. A wooden bench and a cold stone wall. In the street. But they'd soon be through. After all, how long does it take for three people to make a *denuncia*? At the **Comisaría** of Castelldefels, exactly one hour and 47 minutes. They sat there, invisible, as an endless parade of police officers sauntered in and out, or dawdled around a few feet away from them, having a cigarette and discussing last night's game. Theresa hadn't committed a crime, but by the time they were allowed in, she was ready to do so. When Francisco dared broach the extraordinary length of their wait, the friendly *agente* snapped back: "Why didn't you make the *denuncia* by telephone. The number's on the door."
And so it was. Only they had been sitting outside in Arctic temperatures so they hadn't seen it. Just so as you know, if you ever need to report something to the police, and don't have time because you have a plane to catch (Theresa and Francisco were flying back to Malaga early the following day), you can call the 24-hour help line on 902 112 102 and then go to the **comisaría** in your home town when you get back to pick up a copy of your statement. The statement is vital for insurance purposes, and for when you reapply for your **DNI**, Social Security card and Spanish driver's licence.

63

Desastre The Spanish are fond of hyperbole, so while earthquakes and plane crashes are unequivocal disasters, so are you if you happen to mislay your keys/wear odd socks/ put diesel in the petrol tank. But it's more than that. You don't know your mobile number, (still) can't programme a VCR, always pick the wrong girl/guy and have about as much organisational wherewithal as Basil Fawlty. Although we all have our occasional losing-it moments, *ser un desastre* is more of an in-the-genes character flaw which affects every aspect of your life, including zero dress sense and zero sense of direction.

You're a total scat, hopeless, in fact, and it's a wonder you can cope with modern life.

Desayuno The Spanish don't really do breakfast. Not at home. El Segundo Desayuno, the Second Breakfast, however, is another story. Crucial to the smooth running of the country, this is when office workers, bank managers and bricklayers *se ponen las pilas* (charge their batteries) after having dashed out of the house at 7am and crawled in traffic for an hour on a cup of reheated coffee and a stale *madalena* (fairy cake minus the wings). Just never try to buy a stamp or arrange a mortgage between nine and 11 in the morning. If you get fed up with queueing for said stamp or mortgage, you can always nip into the nearest bar and join said office workers, bank managers and bricklayers as they tuck into double *cafés con leche*, glasses of brandy or anisette, and toasted rolls the size of small torpedoes drizzled in garlic oil, rubbed with tomato, stuffed with ham and cheese and bacon, or topped with delights such as *sobrasada* (bright red spicy sausage spread) or *manteca colorá con tropezones* (bright orange pork dripping with lumps of fatty pork sticking out of it). On the other hand, you might just prefer a plain old *cruasán* (official don't-want-all-these-bloody-foreign-words-in-our-language spelling of croissant).

Descubierto Discovered! Revealed! Shameful, guilty secret! It's difficult not to feel like a criminal when you start receiving wrist-slapping letters and cautionary phone calls from your bank about your *descubierto*. In fact, if you have a *descubierto* you have an overdraft. To those who went through university in the UK on generous interest-free overdrafts (and relied on them for several years afterwards), it comes as a shock to find that Spanish banks simply do not "arrange" such painless drifts into debt. Here, for being just a few *céntimos* overdrawn, banks slam you with hefty interest payments from day one — plus other charges.

Despistado Close friend of **desastre,** meaning absent-minded, scatter-brained, in a where-did-I-park-the-car (lost count of the times), oh-my-God-I''ve-just-dumped-my-mobile-in-a-cup-of-cold-tea-on-the-bedside-table (brand new hi-tech phone; never recovered), take-both-sets-of-keys-and-lock-your-partner-in-the-house (just the once) kind of way. Also means confused, not sure what's going on, from the verb *despistar*: to throw off the scent, to mislead.

Desplazamiento Another overly pompous and overly long word that costs us all dearly and means the act of moving from one place to another, often in a work-related context. Thus, your electrician/plumber/general *chapucero* (botch-jobber, see **chapuza**) will charge you for displacing himself to your house. As a tourist you will need to use public transport to "displace yourself", i.e to get around.

Destinatario Recipient. Addressee of a letter or parcel. Payee of a draft or bank transfer. Can also be target, of insults, etc. Not to be confused with *el recipiente,* one of those false friends — it's a container or receptacle.

Detalle A little gift, a little something. A nice or thoughtful gesture. A nice touch. ¡Qué detalle! How sweet of her! *Tiene muchos detalles*...he's a very thoughtful person. But what about the expression *al detalle*? It means retail. So, vender *al detalle* means to retail, to sell retail. By the way, it was the architect Ludwig Mies van der Rohe who said: "God is in the details." Don't know what that has to do with Spain, except that he designed a superb pavilion in Barcelona for the 1929 Universal Exhibition which they restored for the 1992 Olympic Games.

Dietas Allowance, travelling expenses. Never having worked as sales reps, we lived here for years, possibly decades, before realising what *dietas* were. Job adverts promised

65

huge commissions "and *dietas*". Presumably, this meant that they paid for your food if you were on a special diet — such corporate compassion and generosity quite knocked us out. In fact, it merely means all expenses are covered.

Diputación As if we didn't have enough to contend with, with all the state, autonomic and municipal bureaucracy (and lots of cushy sinecures for lots of people), in some places there is yet another layer: the *diputación provincial.* Usually translated as "provincial authority or council", it is defined as "a corporation elected to manage and administer the interests of a province". It is also the building where this happens.

Spain's 19th-century administrative division into provinces still holds. In those days, every province had its *diputación provincial,* which had authority over public works, secondary education and welfare services, and acted as an intermediary

66

between the ***municipios*** (municipalities aka boroughs or towns and villages) and the state, and could be very powerful. In the early 20th century, for example, the Diputación Provincial de Barcelona played a major role in Catalan politics, with an ambitious project to create basic infrastructures and to modernise Catalonia.

With the advent of the **Comunidades Autónomas** in the 1970s and 1980s, the role of the *diputación* was greatly reduced. In communities consisting of more than one province, each province has kept its *diputación* although with far fewer powers. In communities consisting of only one province, the *diputación* ceased to exist and its powers were taken on by the autonomous government. *Diputación* members are elected by all the municipalities in each province, and the *diputación* deals with province-wide matters such as roads between towns, joint sewage plants, municipal library networks, environmental management, forest fire prevention and so on, and may collect municipal taxes on behalf of very small town councils.

Dirección Another word whose many meanings took us ages to grasp. Easiest is where you live: your address, and also direction in the which-way-is-it? sense. In the corporate world La Dirección is "The Management", while Dirección (no article) is the name given to the boss's office. When you go to see your bank manager, for example, his or her office door will have "Dirección" emblazoned across it, because that is where the **director/a** of the bank lives (when he's/she's not on a coffee break). Ah, and hopefully, your car will have *dirección asistida* (power steering).

Director/a Apart from being the head of a school, editor of a newspaper, bank manager, company director and film director, a *director/directora* is also the person who waves the baton at the orchestra (*director de orquesta*). Said person is most definitely not a conductor, a *conductor* being the driver of a vehicle.

DNI (deh-eneh-ee) Documento Nacional de Identidad: National Identity Card. Nothing to be afraid of, honest. From the age of fourteen, by law, you must have your ID on you at all times. This can be your passport, a Spanish driver's licence, DNI or your **residencia.** Foreigners from non-ID card-carrying countries like the UK are often shocked (and stumped) when asked for proof of ID when paying by debit or credit card. Far more shocking to us is that any old signature-forging Juan, José or María could use our cards in the UK. The DNI is valid for five years until you are 30 and for 10 years from 30-70. After the age of 70, it's for life. With the new Sexual Identity Law transsexuals are saved the indignity of having their birth name and birth sex contrast with their appearance. The law allows them to change both of these on their DNI and other official documents without the "proof" of a sex change operation.

Doblar To dub. You are never going to persuade the Spanish — highbrow minority excepted — that subtitles have much going for them. In an effort to cut out the morally objectionable, promote all things Spanish AND make cinema accessible to all (with high illiteracy rates many people just couldn't read subtitles), a sizeable and respectable dubbing industry grew up during Franco's rule. As far as most Spaniards are concerned, the voice they hear IS Clint Eastwood, it IS Sean Connery, it IS Laa Laa and Tinky-Winky. Francisco was outraged the first time he heard the real John Wayne. "Oh, but he sounds so wet," he protested, "*Our* John Wayne is much more of an *hombre*." Theresa could see/hear what he meant. As a rule the standard of dubbing is very high. The dubbed Woody Allen almost outWoodies Woody with his irritating nasal whine; Spanish Clint growls in a suitably mean and moody manner; and Harrison Ford still sounds like the sexiest sexagenarian on the planet.

 68 **Domiciliación bancaria** This tongue-twister refers to paying bills (*recibos*) by direct debit. When you sign up for utilities such as phone, water, electricity and so on, you are obliged to give an account number as a matter of course: paying any other way is not an option. Ditto private insurance, social security payments, satellite TV, Internet... It certainly makes things simpler; it also means that they can sneak extra payments through, so watch your statements like a hawk. Check with your bank at the outset what their time limit is to *devolver un recibo* (send back or cancel a direct debit payment: you can do this by instructing them personally or online, with a couple of clicks). But *domiciliación* is not just about shelling out. You will also be asked for an account number to have your salary, tax rebate, social security benefits and insurance payouts transferred directly into your account. Lucky you.

Dominguero Women in unsuitable shoes and posh frocks tottering around historical monuments/natural parks/pretty villages, overly-done up kids in tow, girls in don't-get-me-dirty dresses, fathers and sons in their starched Sunday bests. In a word: Sunday trippers. And beware *domingueros* at the wheel. They have no notion of lane discipline. They will chug past you on the inside lane of the motorway in their beat-up Seat with its heavy burden of mothers-in-law and whining kids, probably a mattress or two on the roof. A few kilometres on you will find them on the hard shoulder, black smoke billowing from their radiator. As you cruise past smugly, wind the window down and yell: "*¡Dominguerooooo!*"

Don/Doña Title showing respect, similar to Señor and Señora. Mercedes, the live-in carer of Theresa's parents-in-law, would never have addressed her elderly and ailing employees as anything other than Don Manuel and Doña Amelia. Even Theresa was Doña Theresa. But Mercedes was from Ecuador, and the Spanish spoken in Latin America retains an air of gushing respectfulness long since lost in Spain.

69

Donostia The lovely city of San Sebastián (inevitably, La Perla del Cantábrico for tourist bumf writers) has three official names that are accepted by its City Council:

Donostia is the official name in **euskera** (Basque).
San Sebastián is the official name in Castilian.
Donostia-San Sebastián is the official name that is used most widely in official documents.

The difficulty with most Basque names (and words in general) is that they're totally unlike their Castilian equivalents. In this case, while at first glance Donostia seems to bear no resemblance to San Sebastian, there is believed to be a connection. The original name of the city founded by the king of Navarra in the 11th century was Sanctus Sebastianus, after the church of that name, which (translated into Basque) was Done Sebastian.

So, it is thought, Done Sebastian evolved thus: Donebastian - Donebastia - Donastia - Donostia. Yet another name for the city is La Bella Easo (Easo was an ancient name mentioned in Roman writings).

Donostiarra Pertaining to San Sebastián. Illustrious *donostiarras* include sculptor Eduardo Chillida and chef Juan Mari Arzak.

Don Quijote *El Ingenioso Hidalgo Don Quixote de la Mancha* (The Ingenious Knight Don Quixote of la Mancha) was written by Miguel de Cervantes Saavedra in two parts (published in 1605 and 1615 respectively). Conceived as a comic satire against the chivalric romances then in vogue, it's considered by many to be the best novel ever written. Don Quijote and Sancho Panza are the original Odd Couple: the bonkers, accident-prone and yet noble hero and the thick but salt-of-the-earth sidekick. *Don Quijote* is absolutely brilliant and very funny. It's been translated into more than 60 languages and published in every imaginable format, from cartoon book to de-luxe scholarly edition to electronic download, so you have absolutely no excuse. Perfect for long-haul flights or when you break your leg on day one of your skiing holiday.

Droguería Not where you buy drugs of any description, not even an aspirin, but rather where you stock up on anything from shampoo, make-up and cockroach-killer, to light bulbs, perfume and bleach. Very much old-fashioned one-off shops. There are no super-slick, Superdrug-style chains offering own-brand products and state-of-the-art sales ploys. There's usually just the one checkout counter, and any more than three customers in the shop and there's a rush on.

Dúplex Sounds like a cross-between a condom and a toilet roll, but is, in fact, the name given to a two-storey flat. But then, apparently it is in (American) English too.

EE.UU. The United States of America, so good they named it twice? E is Estados (States) and U is Unidos (United), which gives us Estados Unidos. But why the double letters? There are other examples: AA.RR. refers to their Royal Highnesses (Altezas Reales), CC.OO. is Comisiones Obreras, one of the country's biggest trade unions, CC.AA are the Comunidades Autónomas, RR.HH are Recursos Humanos (Human Resources) and FF.CC. is for Ferrocarriles (the Railways). Doubling the consonant is just how the Spanish initialise plural nouns.

Embutidos From time immemorial the people of Spain have chopped up pork and seasoned it with salt and spices (paprika, pepper, garlic, thyme, rosemary, cloves, ginger and nutmeg) to make a myriad of wonderful, tasty sausages to see them through the long winter. Some, like *chorizo, longaniza, salchichón* and *sobrasada* are cured, while others, like *morcilla*, are cooked. *Sobrasada* from Mallorca, *salsichón* from Vic (north of Barcelona) and *lacón* from Galicia are some of Spain's best-known *embutidos* that boast the **IGP (Indicación Geográfica Protegida)** The word *embutir* literally means to stuff into, so *embutidos* are stuffed into animal intestines or, nowadays, similar edible synthetic casing. Valerie recalls falling around with laughter at the less-than-stylish logo of the *embutido* business of a client of Enric's. The headed notepaper and business cards featured a nice, smiley, plump cartoon pig, with a balloon coming out of its mouth that said: *"¡Embúteme!* (Stuff me/Make me into sausage)."* They probably went bust before the animal rights people could get on to them. By the way, the Spanish equivalent of "Let them eat cake" is *"Que les den morcilla"*.

71

Emilio True, it's a man's name, but *emilio* is also a Spanglicisation of email — so much less effort than saying *correo electrónico*. When the film *You Got Mail* came out in 1998, starring Tom Hanks and Meg Ryan, the Spanish distributors gave it the title *Tienes un email*. In fact, you'll hear Spanish people refer to non-snail mail in a variety of ways: *emilio, emeil, meil, correo-e* or *correo*. Light years behind the pulse of the public as usual, the **Real Academia** still only admits the homegrown *correo electrónico* or *mensaje electrónico*.

Empadronamiento Registration with your local **ayuntamiento** (town hall). Everyone who lives in Spain is obliged to *empadronarse*, regardless of nationality and whether or not they have a residence permit. It is a requirement for applying for permits, obtaining health care and so on, and also for voting in elections. As resources are allocated on the basis of the number of registered inhabitants on the *padrón municipal*, services can get seriously overloaded in areas where new residents have not bothered to do this.

Enchufe, enchufar Plug, to plug in, and one of the keys to grasping the mechanics of Spanish life. An *enchufe* is not only a lump of pronged plastic needed to start up your computer/ toaster/television, it also comes in the shape of a life-size, strategically situated human being. This flesh-and-blood *enchufe* may work high up in the place where you have applied for a job. He or she may know a specialist you need to see. Or be on the board of governors of a select school. If your *enchufe* is high up enough, you may be able to jump the queue where it matters. Grossly unfair, of course, but no-one ever looks a gift-plug in the prongs.

Entidad bancaria *Entidad* is a body or organisation, and an *entidad bancaria* is a bank. Why not just say *banco*? In general, Spanish words are longer than their English equivalents, the reasons for which belong in the realm of linguistics. You will find both *entidad* and *bancario/a* cropping up in many places: a bank transfer or banker's draft is a *transferencia bancaria*, for example. On your VAT and income tax forms, the bank is called the slightly sinister *entidad colaboradora*. But you don't really believe that Spanish officialese is deliberately designed to bamboozle the public, do you?

Entrada Entrances and entries of all types, the opposite of *salida* (exit). *Entrada* is also a ticket for the cinema, concerts, shows, exhibitions and other events. Sometimes it can be translated by "admission". And it's what you have to pay as a down payment on a purchase.

E.O.I Escuela Oficial de Idiomas The Official School of Languages offers heavily government-subsidised language classes in everything from Japanese to Arabic and, of course, Spanish (and Catalan, Galician and Basque) and English. The price you pay for paying so little are large classes and mostly traditional tuition (i.e. heavy on grammar, low on communication). We're not knocking it, though. If it hadn't been for two years slogging away at the notoriously difficult fifth level, we wouldn't be able to quip things like: "*Cuando ves la barba de tu vecino quemar, pon la tuya a remojar.*" "When you see your neighbour's beard on fire, better put yours to soak."

Erba *"¿Tu coche tiene erba?"* Does my car have whaaat? But it's an English word, says your Spanish friend. *Erba*? Light-bulb moment: "Ah...you mean airbag!" The **Real Academia** has reluctantly accepted the English word, although, it cautions, it should be pronounced "airbág" (aeerBAG), which is impossible for most Spaniards. The custodians of the sacred language, however, would really feel more comfortable with *bolsa de aire* (literal translation) or *cojín de aire* (air cushion) or even *colchón de aire* (air mat or mattress). Their Catalan counterparts opted, perhaps more logically, to render the airbag's function rather than its content in their own purist proposal: *coixí de seguretat* (safety cushion). Meanwhile, everyone goes on about their *erbas* just the same.

Ertzaintza Basque Police Force, created in 1980, following the restoration of democracy. Pronounced something like er-CHAN-cha. Along with Catalonia and Navarra, the Basque Country is the only autonomous community with its own police force. Regarded as "colonial" lackeys by left-wing nationalists, the Ertzaintza have become a target of the terrorist group ETA. On the other hand, Spanish governments have often criticised the Basque Home Office (to whom the Ertzaintza are directly responsible) for being too soft in the fight against ETA.

74

Escalera de vecinos Literally, staircase of neighbours, referring collectively to the often warring inhabitants of a block of flats (both owner-occupiers and tenants, plus **conserje**, if any). The expression evokes images of groups of people, many in pyjamas, quilted dressing gowns and hairnets, shouting and gesticulating across landings, lift-shafts and air-wells. This very Spanish institution with its typical characters and conflicts has been immortalised in the hilarious Antena 3 comedy series *Aquí no hay quien viva*, about an eccentric Madrid *escalera (*well, the first few seasons were brilliant, then they ran out of ideas). Even if your Spanish is non-existent, don't miss it: catch the reruns on the Factoría de Ficción pay channel or buy it on DVD.

Escritura You'll often find this word translated as a deed or title deed, which is certainly right, but *escritura* is really an umbrella term for any kind of public document *(escritura pública)*, of which the deed to a property is just one specific kind, *una escritura de compraventa*, a public document whereby property is transferred. An *escritura* must be notarised by a **notario**. If the buyer is taking out a mortgage, the representative of the bank will also be present at the signing to formalise a second *escritura, la escritura de hipoteca.*

Escriturar This means to record in an *escritura.* So, for example, the *importe escriturado*, or *valor de escrituración* (the price recorded in the *escritura),* is the official price of a property, on which tax will be calculated.

España A lot of people, in particular Catalans, Basques, etc., are not happy about allowing this word to pass their lips, so they say things like "*el Estado Español*" or "*la geografía española*" or "*el territorio nacional*" (they also share the national propensity for long-windedness). This started at the end of Franco's dictatorship, when *la fiebre autonómica* (home rule fever) spread like wildfire, not only amongst the so-called historical nationalities like the Basques, Catalans and Galicians, but also in regions like Extremadura, Andalusia and the Canary Islands. This was a reaction against the diehard centralism of the dictatorship, when all resources were hoovered up by Madrid. The ideal of the glorious unified *patria* founded by the Catholic Monarchs, which Franco had seen as his duty to save, was debunked, to be replaced by España seen as a patchwork of independent nations held together by coercion.

Español Spanish, no? The language of Cervantes and García Márquez, Julio Iglesias and Pedro Almodóvar. But, according to the Spanish constitution, the *español* spoken in Spain is not actually called *español*, but **castellano**. With around 400 million speakers, it is usually rated as the third most spoken language in the world. However, while it is usually ranked third in number of speakers after Mandarin Chinese and English, some sets of statistics put Hindi third and Spanish fourth — and some even put Spanish just ahead of English. But then, it must be really difficult deciding whom to include and counting all those hundreds of millions of heads. By the time you've finished and processed the data, it's all changed, hasn't it?

Spanish is spoken in Cuba, the Dominican Republic, Puerto Rico, Mexico, Guatemala, El Salvador, Honduras, Nicaragua, Costa Rica, Panama, Colombia, Venezuela, Ecuador, Peru, Chile, Bolivia, Argentina, Uruguay, Paraguay, the Philippines, Spain, Andorra, Morocco, Belize, Equatorial Guinea and the USA. Interestingly, thanks to the spiritual authority of the **Real Academia,** which works in close conjunction with its counterparts in the other Spanish-speaking countries, the same standard spelling rules are applied throughout the world (unlike English and Portuguese). This is a tremendous advantage, for example, for the publishing industry.

Estanco Tobacconist´s, and so much more. The word *estanco* originally meant a tax *(impuesto)* levied to establish a crown monopoly. Our local *estancos* sell fags, designer lighters, ashtrays, newspapers and magazines, multi-ride transport tickets, postcards, Chupa Chups, batteries, lottery tickets, basic office supplies, phone cards and stamps. They also offer a choice of four dog-eared birthday cards (not big on card-sending, the Spanish). An estanco is the ONLY place you can buy stamps apart from the Post Office, and since it acts as a kind of Government stationer's it is also the place you will be sent to buy *timbres de estado,* 19th-century-looking revenue stamps needed to complete strange bureaucratic transactions. Not to be confused with *estanque* (pond).

Estop At the corner of all dodgy non-traffic-light junctions you will find the international red-and-white "Stop" sign. But in spoken Spanish it carries an extra syllable: e-stop. All English and other foreign loan words beginning with an "s" and followed by a consonant are written and/or pronounced in this way. Some examples are: *estárter* (ingeniously, the choke on a car), *estríper* (stripper) *esmoquin* (dinner jacket, from smoking jacket), *escáner, estrés, esvástika, esnob, eslip* (underpants), *espray, eslogan*, and the famous musicians Esting, EspringEsteen and Rod Estewart.

Euskadi The Basque country. In Castilian, el **País Vasco**. Both terms are the official names of the Basque autonomous community, formed by the provinces of Vizcaya, Guipúzcoa and Álava (formerly known in Spanish as the Provincias Vascongadas, an antiquated term still used by many). Euskadi has its own police force (the **Ertzaintza)**, education and health systems, and Basque radio and TV stations. Its capital is Vitoria-Gasteiz.

77

Euskera The Basque language (known as *euskara* in Basque) which is spoken by around 700,000 people in the Basque autonomous community, where it has been co-official with Castilian since 1979. It is also spoken in part of Navarra, and the French Basque Country. Basque is an "isolate": it has no demonstrable relationship with any other known language living or dead, although attempts have been made, some scientific, some totally way out, to relate it to Sumerian/Etruscan/Middle Earthish/Martian/Klingon/you name it. What we can say is that the ancestor of Basque was spoken in western Europe before the ancestors of all the other modern western European languages arrived. Euskera is watched over by the Euskaltzaindia (Academy of the Basque Language).

Excelentísimo Evidently the Spanish just love long-winded titles for their own sake, which is why many **ayuntamientos** (town councils) — and not necessarily those of big cities — like to call themselves *"Excelentísimo"*, abbreviated to *"Excmo"*.

Expediente It really took Valerie years, possibly decades, to realise that *un expediente* is simply a dossier, file, record, as in *Expediente X* (The X Files). Why did she have so much trouble with this word, which to her sounds sinister and threatening? Probably because her husband Enric was a lawyer, so she first learned it in its specialised meaning of disciplinary proceedings or measures, as in "han abierto un expediente a mi cliente" (they've started proceedings against my client). For the sake of brevity, the verb *expedientar* is also used to mean to take disciplinary measures against. But the normal word still makes her feel as if Big Brother is watching her, possibly because it always evokes feelings of bureaucracy-induced helplessness. When her son Eduard needed last summer's marks from Uni to apply for a grant from a private foundation, they logged into his online *expediente académico,* only to find that they couldn't download or print off individual parts of it. So off Eduard went to Uni, where the bureaucrats demanded 19 euros for a printout. No way. He and Valerie finally managed to print the whole thing (four years of it) off the Net and highlighted the relevant bits. It didn't look very official - but he got the grant!

Extremeño Extremaduran, also called *ehtremeñu* or *castúo,* is one of the 13 living languages of Spain. It is spoken in parts of Extremadura, the poorest region of Spain, and in the south of Salamanca province in neighbouring Castilla-León. In fact *extremeño* includes several local variations, which are technically classified by philologists as dialects of Astur-Leonese (see **bable**). It is spoken by an estimated 200,000 people and understood by another 500,000; however, most of these are over 40, and there has been no attempt to teach the language in schools. At the end of 2003, a group of Extremadura writers and academics set up APLEx (the Asociación Estudio y Divulgación del Patrimonio Lingüistico Extremeño) to defend, promote and celebrate all the linguistic variations of the region. One of their current projects is to compile a comprehensive online sound archive. In the late 19th century the famous poet José Maria Gabriel y Galán made the first attempt at a written version of *extremeño* and today several books are published in the language every year. A copy of the Spanish Constitution translated into *extremeño* was presented in October 2004 at the II Congreso del Habla Extremeña. Article 3, 3 states: *"La riqueza 'e loh dihtintut mouh de palral d'Ehpaña, eh un patrimoniu cultural qu'ebi sel rehpetáu y protehíu 'e mou ehpecial.* (The richness of the different linguistic modalities of Spain is a cultural heritage which shall be specially respected and protected)."

Fabla aragonesa *L'aragonés ye una luenga románica, isto ye una luenga naxita de o latín. Por ixo, ye chirmana de o castellano, catalán, franzés, ezetra.* Translation: Aragonese is a Romance language, that is a language that developed from Latin. So it is a sister to Castilian, Catalan, French, etc. Known colloquially as *fabla*, it's spoken or at least understood by an estimated 35,000 people in northern Aragon, although no reliable census has been made. While the language is protected by the Statute of the Autonomous Community of Aragon, its presence at the institutional level and in the school curriculum is practically non-existent. The 1970s saw the establishment of unified spelling rules and a standard grammar, and the emergence of a new literature. Now in the written media Aragonese has a stronger presence, and is enjoying a revival, with a number of organisations of native speakers working to promote it — or rather to save it from extinction. It's on the Unesco Red Book endangered list, which was last updated in 1999. But things may be looking up. Wikipedia, the burgeoning, free online encyclopaedia, has more than 1000 articles in the Aragonese language. If you're really into adopting a language to save it from extinction (why not - you'd adopt a panda or a child in Africa, right?) there's a course at http://es.geocities.com/cursetaragones. And it's great fun. As the rallying cry of the Council for Fabla goes: *Chuntos por l'aragonés!* Together for Aragonese!

Factura Invoice or bill, but not in a restaurant. One of the key issues you need to understand in Spain is whether you get to pay *con o sin factura*. Let's face it, so much business is done here in cash, under the table, in particular with **autónomos**

81

(self-employed). *Con factura* (with an invoice) means you will be issued an official invoice with income tax, VAT etc, and the price will be bumped up to cover the cost of the hassle. Or, to put it another way, if you agree to do the deal *sin factura* (without an invoice), you get a discount. If you want a proper *factura* from your dentist, for example, so you can claim it against tax, you will end up paying more anyway. Many **autónomos** are quite brilliant at negotiating these swings and roundabouts. "We'll do the kitchen cupboards *sin factura*, but the marble tops I'll have to do *con factura*, because the marble top guy invoices me, but if you pay in cash we can either give you a discount on the bathtub or do a *factura* for only half the amount of the tiles, so you only pay half the VAT..." Trust them. They know what they're doing.

Fala Long ago in the Middle Ages, a king of León punished a group of subjects (possibly Galicians) by sending them to the wild frontier, in what is now the province of Cáceres, where they might obtain their pardon by defending the kingdom against the Moors. Starring Mel Gibson and Brad Pitt. No, actually, it's just a possible explanation of why, in an isolated valley in northwestern Extremadura near the border with Portugal, a language closely related to Galician, called *fala*, has been preserved. Also known as *a fala de xálima*, *galaico-extremeño* and the derogatory *chapurreáu* (*chapurrear* means to speak badly), *fala* is spoken in Valverdi du Fresnu, As Ellas and Sa Martín de Trebellu by about 10,500 people, around half of whom live permanently in the Val de Xálima or Val du riu Ellas; the rest have moved away but return home every summer. *Fala*, without a unified writing system, appeared to be doomed, with Castilian making ever greater inroads. But the Fala i Cultura Association succeeded in getting the EU to recognise it as a Minority Language, and in 2001 the Extremadura government recognised the language as a cultural asset worthy of protection. The European-funded project *"A fala na escuela"*

aims to teach *fala* in schools and develop press workshops, popular games, theatre, cultural visits, traditions and legends. And so they should. After all, languages are what Unesco calls our intangible heritage.

Familia numerosa In these days of the declining birthrate (Spain's is the lowest in Europe, after Italy), if you have three or more children you are classified as a large family, and are entitled to certain allowances, grants and tax relief. "Only three?" says Francisco, who comes from a "real" *familia numerosa* of 14. When you get married in Spain, you receive a *libro de familia* (a family record book). In go your mugshots, and then when you have children you add their photos too. In order to claim the allowances, your children must live at home, be under 21 and be economically dependent on you. With 14 in the family, updating the **García** *libro de familia* became a leviathan task requiring two group photos in order to get everybody in. Then, of course, two or three of the older Garcías were always absent, working away from home, or getting into trouble somewhere. So, explains Francisco, his father (a colonel in the army) used to rope in the neighbours and get them to stand in for whoever was missing. In return, they'd be allowed to use the *libro de familia* so they they could travel free on the buses and so on. When his Irish sister-in-law came to stay, they just used to pass her off as one of his sisters. Some things never change. See **paro**.

83

Farmacia Pharmacy, identified by a flashing green cross. This, of course, is where you buy prescription and over-the-counter drugs. Here, too, you can hire baby scales and crutches, weigh yourself, order Scholls sandals, check your blood pressure, and buy pregnancy kits and nicotine patches. The *farmacias* have fought tooth and nail to maintain their monopolies — and horrendous prices — on such things as baby food and tampons, and once upon a time were the only places you could buy these things. It used to be dead easy to get prescription drugs without a prescription (*receta*) from your friendly local *farmacéutico/a*, but now they're tightening up.

To get a licence to open a *farmacia*, you have to be both a qualified pharmacist and have the requisite capital, an archaic monopolistic system which, say its critics, stifles initiative and competition and the career prospects of large numbers of pharmacy graduates. The autonomous governments decide when and where to grant new licences, the criterion apparently being the number of inhabitants to be served. In Barcelona (one of the densest cities in the world, in terms of how many people are squashed in per square metre), there seems to be a *farmacia* on every other corner, with many open till 10pm, and some 24/7. Out of town, they may be few and far between, each serving a number of villages, scattered farms and dwellings, as in El Solsonès, Catalonia's most sparsely populated **comarca**. However, in Theresa's village, although there are no shops and no bars, there is a doctor's surgery and a *farmacia* in someone's hall. If the pharmacist's not there, no problem. You simply knock on the door and her elderly mother appears, urging you to "just help yourself to what you need off the shelf".

Feria What exactly is the difference between a *feria* and a *fiesta*? Good question. A *fiesta*, of course, is a party, and also a public holiday, as in *"el dia 1 de mayo es fiesta"*. A *feria* is a fair: a trade fair, a village fair, a fairground. But often it coincides with the biggest *fiesta* of the year — thus, in Catalonia the *festa major* of a town, village or neighbourhood is also its *feria*.

Ferretería A *ferretería* sells everything from nuts and bolts to chainsaws and liquidisers to *paella* pans and mosquito netting. In other words, it's an old-fashioned, family-owned hardware store-cum-ironmonger´s. Seemingly resistant to new-fangled retail techniques, like shopping baskets, navigable aisles (or even aisles), jolly uniforms and check-out desks, most remain cluttered and poky, with personal counter service from knowledgeable *caballeros* in brown overalls. For the DIY enthusiast, it's like a sweet shop of old: I'll have 10 *tornillos* (regular screws), eight *alcayates* (type of hook), eight *tacos* (plastic peg-things for hooks to go in), and five *cáncamos* (another type of screw), *por favor*. And you'll still get change from a euro. Also the place to get keys cut. It takes years to master the vocabulary of DIY in Spanish, so until you know what *tornillos, alcayates, cáncomos* and *tacos* are, you'd better take along a sample when you ask for five of each.

Ficha One of the great all-purpose words meaning anything from an index card to a file to a domino to a gambling chip to a tiddlywinks counter. Your *ficha médica* is your medical records, your *ficha policial* is your police record, and the *ficha técnica* of your DVD player/talking bathroom scales/digital wok are the technical specifications. In addition, you will hear variants of the word ad nauseam in those noisy football conversations that do not end, alas, with the end of the season, but rather burst forth with renewed vigour; *fichar* means to sign up, *un fichaje* is a signing or signee, and *la ficha* is the signing-on fee or contract. *Un buen fichaje* is a good catch: employee, team mate, or husband.

Finde Weekend for those under 25, and for those who still think they are. From *fin de semana*, but hey, **colega** (think Neil from *The Young Ones*), what a mouthful, five whole syllables...

Finisterra In **gallego,** Fisterra. The westernmost point of Spain on the Costa da Morte in northwest **Galicia**, once believed to mark the end of the known world. Derived from the Latin, *finis-terræ*, literally "land's end". In fact, the westernmost point of Continental Europe is Cabo da Roca, in the Lisbon district of Portugal. Nonetheless, for centuries people believed that if you sailed forth from Cabo Finisterra, you would eventually drop into a large black hole and be gobbled up by strange phantasmagorical creatures. Before you got to the nasty beasts, though, you would sail over the waters where the mythical city of Duyo lay buried — destroyed by God, apparently, as a punishment for the indifference showed by its heathen inhabitants when Saint James turned up to spread the gospel back in the first century.

Finisterra also marks the true end of the **Camino de Santiago** or Way of St. James. In 1492, the Dominican Felix Faber of Ulm published his work on the famous Camino, dividing the journey into 38 stages between his town and Santiago de Compostela. He added a 39th stage from Santiago to Finisterra, declaring: "Beyond Finis Terrae the World ends, and there begin the waters upon which no-one should ever venture." Sound advice. Over the centuries, despite the presence of the Finisterra lighthouse, hundreds of boats have smashed against the rocks or been sucked into the swell around the headland. Every wave, it is said, carries the soul of a sailor who has died there. Hence the name, Costa da Morte: Death Coast. The worst recorded shipwreck occurred on November 28, 1596, when 20 vessels of the Spanish Armada fleet were sunk in a violent storm, killing 1,706 sailors. More recently, the treacherous waters swallowed up the thousands of birds and sea creatures that perished in the Prestige oil tanker disaster in November 2002.

Fiscal Another strike-dread-into-the-heart word. *Fiscal* means pertaining to tax. An asesor fiscal, for example, is a tax consultant, el año fiscal is the tax year, and desgravación fiscal is tax relief. Confusingly, *el fiscal* is also what Brits call the public prosecutor and Americans the district attorney. Hear it in all those thrilling courtroom battles in dubbed movies and TV soaps. *"¡Obyección!"* *"¡Obyección sostenida, señor fiscal!"*

Footing, hacer To go jogging. Theresa's English students always eyed her most sceptically when she told them that people don't go footing in Britain. "Foot" and "–ing", they're both English, aren't they? What's the problem? And you can see their point. After all, the Spanish have happily adopted and bastardised scores of other genuine -ing words. *Un camping* is a camp-site; un parking, a car park; *hacer un planning,* to draw up a plan; and *hacerse un piercing,* to get a hole drilled through a body part. Why couldn't they just say *hacer jogging* and be done with it? Try pronouncing the word as it reads phonetically in Spanish. Anyone for "ggghogghing"? Despite its English components, the word *footing* actually came into Spanish from the French.

Freiduría Fish-and-chip shop without the chips where seafood is sold by weight. Especially popular in Cádiz and Sevilla. There's nothing like wolfing down a coneful of crisp, deep-fried prawns, squid, baby soles, **boquerones** and chunks of succulent cod or *rosada* (white fish).

87

Funcionario Government employee. If a machine or a system works well, it is said to *funciona bien. Funcionarios*, on the other hand, famously don't, or rather do, but as little as possible. A great many people dream of being *funcionarios*.

They study long and hard to become one by passing their **oposiciones** (competitive exams for government jobs). The pay is not brilliant, but the benefits are great and the hours a dream: 8 am–3 pm with written-in-stone coffee breaks, and reduced hours on Fridays and in the summer. Best of all, short of committing serial murder, it is virtually impossible to get fired or laid off. All of this makes for a comfortable and complacent workforce that is long on laid-back and short on sweetness and light. Jokes about the so-called *mentalidad de funcionario* abound. Like this one, posted on the web site of the Junta de Andalucía: "My Paco's a *funcionario* in the Junta. You should see how fast he is — he leaves work at three, and by two he's had lunch and is having his siesta."

Futbolín What have the Spanish ever done for us? Apart, that is, from inventing the first torpedo-firing, electric-powered submarine, Chupa Chups, the mop, the Molotov cocktail, the auto-gyro, cigarettes and the laryngoscope? Well, they gave the world a top-class, not-quite-yet-an-Olympic-sport: *futbolín*, or table football. During the Spanish Civil war, 17-year-old Alejandro Finisterre was injured in a bomb attack during the siege of Madrid by Nationalist forces. During his convalescence in a hospital near Montserrat, Catalonia, the young inventor first dreamt up a sheet music turning device for the piano. Then, feeling sorry for the children who had been crippled during the war, he set about fashioning a handsome table football game, using wooden figures, metal bars and a cork ball.

What happened to Finisterre and his invention after the Civil War ended is surely worthy of some film director's time and money. Forced to flee to France, on foot, across the Pyrenees, our young hero just had time to pack a tin of sardines, a couple of favourite plays and the patent for his game. Unfortunately, it rained solidly during his 10-day hike and the patent (which he had registered in Barcelona in 1937) turned to squelch. Shortly afterwards, he emigrated to Guatemala, where, undeterred, he continued to perfect his beloved futbolín. Sales were doing brilliantly in Latin America, but then in 1954 Castillo-Armas invaded Guatemala in a CIA-backed coup, and Finisterre was kidnapped (apparently, because of his Republican connections) and was put on a plane back to Madrid. Ever resourceful, he threatened the pilot mid-flight, and hijacked the plane. Following a thwarted attempt to set up his business in the USA (the mafia wanted a huge cut of the profits), he settled in Mexico, where everybody immediately started copying his idea. Finisterre finally threw in the towel, and turned full-time to writing and publishing. Meanwhile, the manufacturers who had made his prototype back in Spain, in Valencia, had grown rich, and on his return to Spain during the 1960s, the writer, poet, entrepreneur and inventor was astounded to see that futbolín had virtually become a national sport.

89

Galicia Also called the romantic sounding Galiza (in **gallego**). Autonomous Community in the northwestern corner of Spain, formed by the provinces of A Coruña, Lugo, Ourense and Pontevedra. And the archipelago of the Cies Islands (El Faro, Monteagudo and San Martiño islands), the Ons Archipelago (Ons Island and Onza Island — honest), the Sálvora archipelago (Sálvora, Viontia and Sagres) and a further sprinkling of islands, Cortegada, Arosa, the Sisargas, or Malveiras. No, we had no idea, either. But don't you just love the names. Pub quiz question writers, take note. Most of these islands belong to the Parque Nacional de las Islas Atlánticas. Tragically and ironically, only six months after being declared a national park, the area was hit by the oil slick from the Prestige tanker which sank off the Spanish coast in 2002.

The Celtic influence in Galicia is very strong, and the whole place is as far from the stereotypes of Spain as you could imagine. Valerie visited Galicia many years ago with a Welsh friend, who never stopped exclaiming about how Welsh everything seemed: the grey stone constructions, the small dark people, the sing-song lilt that Gallegos bring to the Castilian language, their love of singing in choirs... The Galicians are also heavily into bagpipes, we might add. Galicia is the rainiest part of Spain and, therefore, gorgeously green. It's also one of the poorest, and like wet, emerald Ireland, has suffered mass emigration, to such an extent that there are *gallegos* in every corner of the globe, and even, it is said, on the moon. In Argentina, Colombia and Uruguay the word *gallego* is synonymous with a person born in Spain or of Spanish descent.

Gallego The language of **Galicia**, called *galego* in Gallego itself. This is a Romance language very closely related to Portuguese, and currently spoken by over three million people in the Autonomous Community of Galicia, where it is co-official with Castilian. In the Middle Ages, when it was virtually indistinguishable from Portuguese, *gallego* was the literary language of poetry, not only in its own territory, but in Castilian-speaking areas too. Under Franco's dictatorship, although it managed to survive, particularly in rural areas, in the cities it was subject to massive inroads from Castilian. In 1982 the Real Academia Galega and the Instituto da Lingua Galega established a unified set of rules, and the following year the Galician Parliament passed the Lei de Normalización Lingüística de Galicia. Since then the language has been promoted in all walks of life, with vigorous efforts at "de-Spanishification". According to a recent study, *gallego* is known by about 80 per cent of the population. Alongside Italian it is the earliest written Romance language, with texts dating to more than a century before Castilian. Recently the oldest extant document written in *gallego*, dating to 1228, was discovered by a University of Santiago de Compostela researcher. Outside Galicia, the language is spoken by about 50,000 people in western Asturias, 20,000 in León and 2,500 in **Zamora** — and by the huge numbers of *gallegos* living abroad.

Rosalía de Castro (1837-1885), a native of **Santiago de Compostela**, wrote the first important poetry in *gallego* since the 13th century, ushering in the movement known as the Rexurdimento (Galicia's literary, cultural, political and historical Renaissance) and reestablishing *gallego* as a language of literature and culture. The date she published her first collection of poetry, *Cantares gallegos*, May 17 1863, is commemorated every year as the Día das Letras Galegas (Galician Literature Day), and is an official holiday in Galicia. Every year it is dedicated to a different Galician writer.

Genio
Gitano
Gestor El Gordo *Galicia* **Gestor** Goyas Galicia Goyas
El Gordo Grúa Gitano
Guiri

García The most common surname in Spain (1,378,000), followed by Fernández, González and Rodríguez. Among the 1,378,000 are Francisco and his 13 brothers and sisters together with several thousand nephews and nieces and aunts and uncles. He and Theresa are due to marry, so then Theresa can "grow" an extra surname and join the García gang herself, by becoming Theresa O'Shea de García (see *apellido*).

Generalitat Why are the governments of Catalonia and the Comunitat Valenciana called "the generalty" — generalty of what? It turns out that strictly speaking the Generalitat is not the government itself, but the system of government. This goes back to the 13th century, to the medieval courts of the ancient principality of Catalonia and the kingdom of Valencia respectively, both of which were abolished in 1715 by Philip V. Be that as it may, Generalitat horror stories are rife in the two communities, where the G word is synonymous with a huge lumbering bureaucracy whose right hand doesn't know what its left is doing. Worn out with masses and masses of paperwork, repeat visits and hours of queuing, you wonder whether the right to **autonomía** was simply the right to have your bureaucracy ineptly lumbering closer to home instead of having to go to Madrid every time you needed something sorted. When Valerie was a translator, she was told that the Generalitat de Catalunya took more than a year to pay for translations and other freelance commissions, so she refused to have anything to do with them. As we write this, a correspondent reports from Valencia that she still hasn't received her young persons' rent subsidy for 2004. One sweltering summer in Barcelona, a musician friend of Valerie and Enric's nearly went berserk with the clattering and whirring of air conditioners on the roof of a nearby building. Why didn't he report them for noise pollution to the environment department, they asked, with suitably righteous indignation. "They ARE the environment department!" he wailed. "Of the Generalitat!"

93

Genio You would perhaps expect *genio* to mean genie or genius. And it does. But it is also used to describe someone's spirit or character. Thus we get the oft-used *tener mal genio* (to be a bad-tempered, irascible old cow, or bull).

Gestión This has two main meanings: management, as in, for example, *gestión de residuos* (waste management) and a negotiation, a sorting out, a bureaucratic or administrative errand, a bit of business. *Hacer gestiones* can range from solving a minor problem with a bank to major negotiations like pulling troops out of Iraq, and may imply and sometimes require pulling strings. When your building permission gets held up, your architect does *gestiones* to get it through. Lawyers do *gestiones* to get their clients out of prison or settle cases out of court. A football club does *gestiones* to sign Becks or similar. If you don't feel like answering the phone, and your clients no longer believe the one about being in a meeting, get your secretary to say "she/he's out *haciendo gestiones*". And, it's understood, God only knows when you'll be back.

Gestoría (HHestoREEYa) Firm or office of a **gestor**.

Gestor You've been sitting for hours on a plastic chair at, say, the tax office, glued to the screen for your number (probably three figures) to come up, and you see all these guys with bulging document cases being let through even though they've only just arrived. An indignant murmur ripples through the crowd, glances are exchanged, the murmur rises to a crescendo... You kick yourself and swear that next time, however high the fee, you will hire a *gestor* yourself: a professional knower of the often tangled ropes, a hands-on doer of **gestiones**, tedious paperwork, tax returns and accounts, expert sorter-out of bureaucratic hassles of every kind. Believe us, a good one is worth his/her fees in gold. By the way, for online **gestiones**, you will still need your *gestor* on the phone to talk you through the most user-unfriendly websites on the Net.

Gilipollas (GghhilliPOLyass) Colloquial word meaning dickhead, jerk, prat. Even though it contains the word *"polla"* (willy), it is fairly mild (the other half of the word, *gili*, is from the gypsy **caló** language, and means innocent, naive). The small daughter of one British friend went down in Spanglish howler history when she dismissed a schoolmate as a "sillypollas". *Una gilipollez,* by the way, is a f***ing stupid thing to say or do.

Gilipuertas Twit. The *pollas* part of the word is discreetly replaced.

Gitano Gitanos are a Roma people who live in the south of France, Spain and Portugal. In France they are *gitans* and in Portugal *ciganos*. In Spain they speak **caló**, a language based on Romany vocabulary but with Spanish grammar. Like the English word "gypsy", gitano comes from *Egiptiano*, as they were once thought to have originated in Egypt. It is now believed, however, that the gypsies migrated to Europe from India around the 11th century. Records show that they arrived in Spain during the 15th century. Bad timing. During the Catholic Reconquest, after 1492, along with the Jews and the Muslims, the *gitanos* were earmarked for persecution, assimilation or expulsion. For the next 300 years every attempt was made to destroy them as a recognisable cultural group. Under Franco, like the **quinquis**, they were harassed and persecuted and forced to abandon their semi-nomadic ways. Today, despite the government's pro-*gitano* initiatives, they are still very much an underclass, and are subject to fierce stereotyping and discrimination. Of the estimated 650,000 *gitano* population, almost half live in Andalusia, and in 1996 the Andalusian parliament declared November 22 "El Día de los Gitanos Andaluces", to commemorate the date of their arrival in the region in 1462. The other major gypsy populations are centred in Extremadura, Madrid, Valencia and Catalonia, while the north of Spain has the smallest number.

95

Traditionally, many of Spain's great flamenco artists have been *gitanos,* like the late great Camarón, flamenco-rock group Ketama, flamenco-pop singer Rosario Flores, and the internationally acclaimed dancer Joaquín Cortés. Ironically, while their success and influence in the world of music and dance helps build a more positive image, it also reinforces old stereotypes. "It seems we either spend all day dancing or fighting with knives and rifles," complained one interviewee in a feature on "middle-class *gitanos*" in the *El País* newspaper (March 12, 2006). An estimated 80 per cent of all gypsies have, in fact, integrated into society. They work (mostly as market-traders), send their children to school, they don't live in slums and they are neither flamenco artists nor drug-traffickers. But, although illiteracy has halved since 1977, it still stands at 40 per cent. Only one per cent complete the compulsory phase of secondary education (until the age of 16), while university students from a gypsy background account for barely 1000 out of a total of 1.5 million.

96

El Gordo The Big One, the Fat One. The most famous and financially fattest lottery in the world. There are masses of big money prizes, now totalling over two billion euros, with payout for the winning number standing at a breezy three million euros. Each number is divided into 10 equal parts, called *décimos,* and each number belongs to a series, of which there are 10. Clear as mud, right? Basically, if you hold one of the 100 *décimos* of the winning number you can wave goodbye to your clapped-out Seat Panda. Despite the cost of the tickets (20 euros a bash), it is estimated that 90 per cent of the population succumb to the temptation of The Fat One. On the morning of the draw (December 22) any local bar is the place to be, with everyone glued to the TV screen, clutching their tickets, as the winning numbers are read out in sing-song style by children from the San Ildefonso school.

What is unique about the Christmas Lottery is that the prize money gets spread around so far and so wide. An estimated one out of every three tickets attracts a prize of some description. Entire villages, blocks of flats, factories, offices, bars, hairdressers, branches of football supporters clubs and political parties buy up a series of numbers and sell or give away the *décimos* and *participaciones* (more affordable fractions of *décimos*). You dare not be left out. We hadn't been in our village long when one December night, a neighbour came knocking at our door on a mercy mission. "It's just that you're the only ones without a ticket. We'd hate you to be the only ones who don't win." So we weren't. And we didn't.

Gorro/gorra We can never remember the difference, but *gorro* is the general word for a hat worn close to the head, while *gorra* refers specifically to a peaked cap. Nothing to do with heads and hats, but if you go through life *de gorra*, you're a freeloader. *De gorra* means gratis, for free. Used in particular with *vivir, comer, viajar*. *Gorrear* is to scrounge, sponge, freeload, and the person who does it is *un gorrero*.

Goyas Hollywood has its Oscars, France its Césars, Britain its Baftas, and Spain its Goyas. But instead of a sleek golden statue looking like a doll for extraterrestrials, Spain's lauded directors and actors receive a chunky bronze bust of the great Spanish painter Francisco de Goya on a bad hair day. The prizes, all 28 of them, are conferred by the Academia de las Artes y Ciencias Cinematográficas de España, and awarded in a ceremony around the end of January. Like the Oscars, the Goyas are not without their critics. Over the years, many top directors, such as Carlos Saura and Pedro Almodóvar, have criticised (and boycotted) the awards because of what they see as an unfair voting system. Despite having won scores of international awards for his work (including two Oscars), Almodóvar has only

Genio

Gestor

Galicia

Grua

stor El Gordo Gitano Goyas Grúa

Galicia Goyas

El Gordo Guiri

ever won two Goyas. In 2005, when his film *Mala Educación (Bad Education)* went away empty-handed, he announced his departure from the Academy. (The voting procedure for the awards is under review.)

Granja The word means a farm, but in Catalonia it's also a small cafe or teashop, where kids and seniors go for **desayuno** and **merienda**. A sort of milk bar where you can buy/consume dairy products and sugary cakes and buns, the *granja* used to be the only place you could get hold of fresh whipped cream (*nata montada*) before they started selling the stuff in aerosols in supermarkets.

Grogui Marvellous spelling of a good old sea-faring word. Meaning groggy.

Grúa Ostensibly a crane, but also the name of the truck that tows away your illegally parked car. The *grúa* drivers work in conjunction with the local police and are held in about as much public esteem as our own dear traffic wardens. Quick, *viene la grúa*, the tow-away truck is coming. Too late? Never mind, nice men that they are, they'll have left you a calling card: a pretty orange triangle stamped with the removal time and a telephone number. Expect to pay anywhere between 60 and 135 euros to get your car out of the *depósito de coches* (car pound), plus an extra fee per day. But the *grúa* isn't all bad. When your car breaks down and there's nothing between you and three lanes of supersonic traffic but a small orange hazard triangle, a quick call on the mobile and a knight or two in regulation uniform will soon be there to tow you to safety.

Guardería Short for *guardería* infantil: nursery, creche, day-care centre. As its name suggests, it's a place where babies and children are *guardados* (kept, watched, or to be cynical, put away).

Guardia Civil In a country where there are so many levels of police (national, autonomic, local), at least you know the Guardia Civil are the Guardia Civil, with their distinctive green uniforms, peaked caps, fabulous knee-high boots, and Chevrolet-type patrol cars that zip up and down the highways and hang out at junctions to catch helmet-less motorcyclists and over-the-limit drivers. Gone, however, are the days of the *tricornios,* the old three-cornered hats, which are now only worn in official ceremonies. And pairs of guards no longer patrol the streets with sub-machine guns, terrifying the life out of the population.

Despite their reputation for brutality and torture during the Franco dictatorship, and despite the failed coup by Lieutenant Colonel Antonio Tejero Molina in 1981 with 300 of his men, the Guardia Civil have successfully been given a new image. Their jurisdiction often overlaps that of other police forces; however, they are exclusively in charge of intercity traffic, the highways and ports, the prevention and prosecution of fraud, the protection of the natural environment, contraband and explosives.

99

The Guardia Civil are the subject of many jokes. They are usually depicted as one or all of the following: dim-witted ignoramuses, racist or homosexual (because they still patrol in pairs).

Joke 1

A Civil Guard patrol car flags down a sports car for reckless driving. One of the guards gets out of the car and asks to see the driver's *papeles*. On reading them, he clicks his heels together, salutes, and waves the vehicle on.

"Who was that?" asks his partner.
"I don't know. But on his paper it said:
'General Motors'." (Groan)

Joke 2

A spaceship lands. Two extraterrestrials get out and find a *tricornio* in the middle of the road.

"What's that?"

"I don't know. What do you think?"

"I don't know either. Such a strange shape."

"Listen, why don't you try it on and see if you can work out what it's for?"

The first extraterrestrial picks up the hat carefully and puts it on his head.

"What is it? What is it?"

"No idea, but you know something? I've got this sudden urge to give you a damn good belting."

Guiri Pronounced "gheeree". Unless you are as dark and handsome as Penélope Cruz or Antonio Banderas, speak the lingo like a native and dress with unfailing style and sophistication, you are bound to be referred to, on countless occasions, as a *guiri*, a white, western foreigner who's probably a tourist and/or who doesn't speak Spanish. Theresa has lived here for 16 years, has a Spanish partner, speaks Spanish fluently, and wouldn't dream of wearing shorts and flip-flops around town in February. However, she is fair-haired and blue-eyed. She looks like a guiri. She gets called a *guiri*. So does her friend Sandra, who, with her thick dark chestnut hair, passes muster until she opens her mouth and her *anglo-andaluz* accent gives her away.

Not all western foreigners are considered to be *guiris*, however. Generally speaking, the guiri is assumed to be British, German, Scandinavian or American. The Italians are not *guiris* (they are just noisy *italianos*), nor the Portuguese, nor the Greeks, nor the French, in part because they share similarities with the Spanish in terms of language, looks, dress sense and culture. The big question, of course, is whether the term is offensive. The **Real**

Academia says it is "colloquial" (rather than "pejorative"), but Theresa's old University of Salamanca dictionary (1996) says it is definitely pejorative and gives us the following example: "*Guiris rojos como gambas se pasean por la playa* (*Guiris* red as prawns walk along the beach)." Well, we've all seen them, haven't we? But the term has a range of connotations and is often used affectionately, as are words like Aussies, Kiwis, Saffas etc. We certainly use it that way ourselves.

The other point to consider is that the current meaning was coined in the 1960s when Spain was slowly opening up to tourism after decades of relative isolationism. For most Spaniards, foreign travel was impossibly remote, and the trappings and comforts of modern life remained out of reach. The exotic *guiri* from northern Europe, with his, and very often her, new ideas, modern clothes and liberal attitudes, was viewed with a mixture of fear and envy. Then we ruined it all by wearing socks and sandals.

101

Güisqui Whisky. The **Real Academia** only grudgingly admits foreign words that have no equivalent in Spanish, and only very grudgingly those that are already totally assimilated into the vernacular. They finally deigned to admit whisky, but only by spanglicising the word beyond recognition to *güisqui* as the Spanish alphabet does not include the letters "w" and "k". Nobody paid a blind bit of notice and went on drinking "whisky", or as they say in Andalusia where syllables and letters are knocked back with the tapas, "wi-ki". Whatever the spelling, it is not a substance to be messed with. Do not under any circumstances invite your Spanish neighbours/new friends around for a meal without a bottle of the stuff (preferably JB, Gghhota Bay) at the ready for an after-coffee *copa.* To be served on ice-cubes the size of yoghurt pots with Seven-Up or Coca-Cola.

H The eighth letter of the Spanish alphabet is pronounced A-tchay. It is always silent at the beginning of a word: hotel is o-TEL; horrible, o-RRI-blay and hola, O-la.

103

Habanera

My grandad went to Cuba
On board the Català
The best war ship
Of the overseas fleet.
The helmsman and the skipper
And fourteen sailors
Were born in Calella
Were born in Palafrugell.

So goes Valerie's literal translation of the *habanera El Meu Avi,* a wallowing-in-nostalgia song known by almost everyone in Catalonia; as it goes on to recount the glorious demise of grandad and all on board while defending the remnants of the empire, audiences at village fetes are urged to wave white hankies. *Habaneras* are typical sailor songs or sea shanties that were brought to Catalonia by fishermen and traders returning from the Caribbean colonies, in particular Cuba, in the 19th century. In 1898 war broke out between Spain and the United States (la Guerra de Cuba, also known as El Desastre del 98) which culminated in the loss of Spain's remaining overseas colonies (Philippines, Puerto Rico and Cuba) — the end of the empire. But the music lived on, in taverns and now as the mainstay of fairs and fetes throughout Catalonia, along with hot rum (see *queimada*), another Caribbean legacy. Named, obviously, after Havana, the capital of Cuba, *habaneras* are sung in harmony, accompanied by guitar, accordion, and bass, by men in striped jerseys and white pants. The *habanera* has its own dedicated festivals, the most famous one being held every July on the beach of Calella de Palafrugell, world *habanera* capital. Listen and wallow here: www.pescadorsdelescala.com

Habilitar Another tricky word for translators, meaning something like "to make suitable", "to fit out". The town hall may say they are going to *habilitar* an area of waste ground as a children's park, or *habilitar* a disused railway as a route for cyclists. If you're brave enough to have your computer software in Spanish, you will soon realise that when a function of a program is *habilitado,* it is operative. Here, the correct translation would be "enabled".

Hacienda Like the Inland Revenue for Brits and the IRS for Americans, this is probably Spain's most panic-inducing word/institution. Pity, because it sounds so dashing, conjuring up pictures of ranches down Mexico way complete with handsome horsemen galloping off into the sunset. "Estate" or "ranch" (when devoted to livestock) is one of the main meanings of the word, from Old Spanish *facienda*, a Latin word meaning literally "things to be done". So *hacienda lechera* is a dairy farm and *hacienda tabacalera* a tobacco plantation. The other main meaning is possessions, property, hence *hacienda pública*

104

meaning public funds. The H-word may refer to the Treasury (Ministerio de Hacienda), the local tax office (Delegación de Hacienda), and "the taxman". *Un inspector de Hacienda* is, of course, the dreaded tax inspector.

Himno Nacional The national anthem, a plodding little number known as *La Marcha Real* (The Royal March) or *La Marcha Granadera*. The authorship of the music, which dates back to the 1760s, remains a mystery, although some historians believe it was composed by Frederick the Great of Prussia. As it is one of the few national anthems not to have any words, sportsmen and women can hold their heads high, their lips free from the need for awkward mumbling. However, at the Davis Cup final in 2003 the Spanish team could only gape in astonishment when the Australians put their foot in it big time by playing the *Himno Riego,* the official anthem of the First and Second Republic (1873-1874 and 1931-1939 respectively). A formal apology was made, but the Spanish officials were most put out and considered the whole thing a huge *provocación.*

105

The Republican anthem was written in honour of General Riego, leader of the liberal uprising against the absolutist Fernando VII in 1820. Apart from the official soldiers-and-glory lyrics, many popular verses have evolved over the years, including one with the famous anti-clerical lines:

> *Si los curas y frailes supieran*
> *la paliza que les van a dar*
> *subirían al coro cantando:*
> *"Libertad, libertad, libertad!"*

> *If the priests and the friars knew*
> *what a hiding they're going to get*
> *They'd climb up to the choir singing*
> *"Freedom, freedom, freedom!"*

Hola We say hello, and they say goodbye. We're used to this now, but it remained weird for a long time. When walking down the street it's only natural to greet someone you know with *"Hola"*. The Spanish, however, get right to the point and despatch you with an *"Adios."*

Hora The magic word. Life becomes so much easier when it clicks that hora is the correct word for appointment. If you want to make one, say: *"Quisiera pedir hora."* However — and this is quite a big however — having an *hora,* even *primera hora,* while relieving you of fighting for a **número** and a place in the queue, doesn't necessarily mean you won't have to endure hours of waiting. *Cita,* a blanket term for appointments of all kinds, is also a date, so better not ask your hairdresser/doctor/dentist/osteopath/psychiatrist, etc. for one unless you really fancy your chances.

Horchata Tiger nut milk. You either love it or you hate it: a thick creamy drink made from crushing the life out of tiger nuts (*chufas*) and mixing with sugar and water. There's nothing quite like an icy-cold glass of the stuff on a pavement-melting day. Served fresh in *heladerías* (ice-cream parlours), where you can also take your own bottles or flasks for a carry-out. Bars sell bottled versions, but there is no comparison. In Spain, tiger nuts, a kind of tuber, are only grown in Valencia, and since 1995 the *chufa de Valencia* has been a **Denominación de Origen (D.O.)** product. According to the web site of the Regulatory Council of the D.O. Chufa of Valencia, tiger nuts are rich in phosphorus, potassium and vitamins C and E. On a more worrying note, the *chufa* powers that be tell us that: "Natural tiger milk can be presented as liquid, hailstorm or congealed." Not to worry. "Hailstorm" is a literal translation of *"granizado"*, which in this case means something like a Slush Puppy, while "congealed" is woeful computer translatese for *congelado,* meaning "frozen".

The story behind how *horchata* got its name is as unlikely as it is entertaining. Back in the 13th century a young village girl offered the king of Catalonia and Aragon a glass of tiger nut milk while he took a rest from fighting against the Moorish army. "Mmm," he said (in Catalan), "*¿Qué és això?* (What's this?)"

"*És leche de chufa* (It's tiger nut milk)," she replied. "*Això no és llet,*" he declared. "*¡Això és OR, XATA!* (That's not milk, it's gold, darling!)" In Catalan "or" is gold, and "xata", pronounced "chata", a term of endearment, like darling. From then on, the drink became known as "*horchata de chufa*". The word "*chufa*", on the other hand, probably comes from a place in Sudan called Chufi, where the tiger nut is thought to have originated several thousand years ago.

Hostia Communion wafer. And so much more. Used as a general sort of damn-and-blast exclamation, depending on the intonation, *hostia* can express everything from surprise and admiration to self-admonishment and pain. In a country where the Church has historically held great power, religion-related swear words and expressions are among the strongest — much stronger than the equivalents of our own "C" and "F" words. That is certainly the case with the surely very-difficult-to-manage *me cago en la hostia* (I defecate on the communion wafer).

Hueco When you're going crazy with toothache and are told there are no **horas** for the next three months, try saying in your most pathetic, grovelling voice: "*Por favor, ¿no me puede encontrar un hueco?*" That is, can't you squeeze me in? A *hueco* is a hole or gap.

107

IBI (eebee) Impuesto sobre Bienes Inmuebles. An annual tax you pay on your property, according to the value of the land on which the property is built *(el valor catastral)*. It is levied locally and varies widely, depending on the municipality you live in. The IBI for Theresa's village house in the Axarquía costs just 62 euros a year, while Valerie pays more than 500 euros for her elegant flat in downtown Barcelona. Not a lot, really, compared with UK council tax. Incidentally, if you own a parking space in a garage you will also pay IBI on that.

Ikastola Basque-language school, committed to recovering and promoting the Basque language and culture. The first (clandestine) *ikastolas* were set up during the Franco regime, and are now integrated into the ordinary school system, some state-funded, others private.

109

Ikurriña The Basque national flag, consisting of a white cross over a diagonal green cross on a red field, patterned after the British Union Jack. The red represents the blood shed by the Basques in their fight for independence, the white is for the Catholic faith and the green for the oak tree of Guernica. (The word is the Castilian version of the Basque *ikurrin*.) The *ikurriña* was the flag of the Basque republic of 1936-37. Banned under Franco and then reinstated as the official flag of the Basque Autonomous Government, now it flies everywhere in the Basque Country, on both the French and Spanish sides.

Ilustre Honourable, sort of, used for certain professional societies. The Ilustre Colegio de Abogados de Madrid or the Ilustre Colegio Oficial de Ingenieros Industriales de Galicia hark back, ever so slightly wistfully, to the lofty esteem in which doctors, lawyers and others who had obtained a professional qualification were held in days less egalitarian than our own.

Ilustrísimo Also honourable. *Su Ilustrísimo* is roughly equivalent to Your Grace (when addressing a bishop, for example).

Impuesto To put it bluntly, tax. Apart from the pronounceable IVA (EEvah: Impuesto sobre el Valor Añadido : VAT), the abbreviations for most Spanish taxes are real tongue-twisters. It has taken us years to get the IRPF (ee erray pay effay) to trip off the tongue (Impuesto sobre la Renta de las Personas Físicas: personal income tax). And, after years of car ownership (and digging in our pockets), we are still barely able to utter any reference to the equivalent of road tax, IVTM (ee oovay tay emmay) or the seriously longwinded Impuesto sobre Vehículos de Tracción Mecánica.

110

IMSERSO Instituto de Migraciones y Servicios Sociales. (Formerly INSERSO, before the incorporation of Migration). The government Department of Social Services, responsible for providing social security, health and economic benefits for Spanish citizens and foreigners. For most people, though, IMSERSO (or INSERSO as most people still call it) conjures up images of coach-loads of partying senior citizens on their way to ballroom dance the night away in Benidorm. Every year, once most Spaniards have had their annual holiday and the kids are back at school, the government offers nearly half a million low-cost holidays to the over-65s, the disabled and various marginal groups. As part of this admirable initiative involving the public and private sectors, pensioners may opt for fun-in-the-sun breaks on the major Costas and islands, cultural trips in the interior, or a fortnight of pampering and medical treatment at a spa. IMSERSO have branches in each province and for any disabled person planning their holiday in Spain, according to

Disability View magazine, they offer "first rate accessibility information".

Indiano Name applied to Spaniards who returned home having made fortunes in Latin America, which Columbus had wrongly identified as *Las Indias*. *Indianos* played an important role in the art and culture of the 19th and early 20th century. Ramón Casas, who revived Catalan painting in the late 19th century and spearheaded the *modernista* movement, was the son of an *indiano* who had made a fortune in Cuba. The renowned *Indiano Quartet* by the 20th-century composer Xavier Montsalvatge was written in memory of the Catalan *indianos*. A lot of *indiano* money was associated with the big names in residential building, like Samà (lovely park near Cambrils on the Costa Dorada) and Güell (Gaudí's patron) in Barcelona and elsewhere. In Sitges, you can actually do an *indiano* tour of fabulous mansions commissioned from Modernist and Art Nouveau architects by returning "*americanos*". There is also a large amount of *indiano* architecture in Asturias. Like the British who sailed to India or Africa to seek their fortune or simply gainful employment, the *indiano* is also a recurring theme in the literature of the period. And, like their British counterparts, most Spaniards didn't come back rich from *Las Indias*.

Indicación Geográfica Protegida (IGP) Officially translated as Protected Designation of Origin. To be awarded an IGP with its distinctive blue-and-yellow seal (the same as the **DOP** but with the relevant wording) there has to be a link with the geographical location in at least one of the stages of production, transformation or elaboration of the product. Spanish IGP goodies include Mallorcan *ensaimadas* (so that's what's in those huge octagonal parcels you see everyone lugging off the planes and ferries from the Balearics), **turrón** from Alicante and Jijona, beans from Asturias, apples from Girona, clementines from the Ebro Valley…

111

INEM Instituto Nacional de Empleo, the National Institute of Employment (or Unemployment, if you're a glass-half-empty sort of person). Your local *oficina de empleo* (sort of job centre and DHSS office combined) is the place you go to *darse de alta en el **paro** (*to sign on the dole) and/or register as unemployed. Forget, however, all notions of user-friendly job centres with large panels of employment offers laid out like a touchy-feely art exhibition. If there is a job that fits your profile, they'll call you to arrange an interview. You are far more likely to find work answering an ad in the newspaper or through a private employment agency.

Inmueble Why *"un inmueble"* should mean a building was something we could never understand. We used to get it mixed up with *un mueble* (a piece of furniture). No, we'd repeat, not an *inmueble,* we're talking about un edificio, *un bloque de pisos, una casa.* Later, when we learned a bit about assets and liabilities and balance sheets, it clicked. *Bienes inmuebles* were immovable assets. Property. Real estate. And *un mueble,* logically, was a thing you could move around. And so the adjective *inmobiliario* refers to real estate. *Una inmobiliaria* may be *una agencia inmobiliaria* (estate agent) or *una empresa constructora* (property developer).

(112)

Interviú Spanglicised spelling of interview, and the steamiest mainstream magazine on the shelves. Apart from hard-hitting, exposé-type journalism, the rag offers a weekly flesh-fest of soap stars, *Big Brother* celebs, TV presenters and sports stars. You'll never see page-three girls in the Spanish newspapers, which tend to be dry and worthy to the point of tedium, but in *Interviú* full frontals abound. One of the curious hallmarks of a country that spent the swinging Sixties and most of the Seventies under a dictatorship is that censorship of any kind is seen as an inherently BAD THING. Hence the likelihood of finding your favourite *Cooking with Tofu* and *Crochet Today*

titles sidled up to *Bondage Babes* and *Perversions Monthly*.

Invitar An extremely important little word. In Spanish, if you invite someone to the cinema, you will definitely be paying. *Te invito* means "I'm paying", "It's my treat". And the Spanish, being a generous lot, do an awful lot of *invitando*. Going Dutch is not the norm and it is actually considered quite *feo* (ugly) if you insist on trying to split a bill for a coffee or a drink or two. At the end of a meal, bill-splitting is normal, but try to avoid saying things like: "I didn't have any wine, Mary didn't have a dessert and my chicken was cheaper than what you all had, so our share of the bill is X euros." Accept any *invitación* gracefully, and next time make sure you reciprocate. Ah, and when it's your birthday don't expect everyone to buy you a drink. It's your birthday, it's your shout.

113

ITV (Pronounced ee-tay-OO-vay). Not a defunct television channel, but Inspección Técnica de Vehículos and the Spanish equivalent of the MOT. On a new car it's four years before you are required to roll up at your local ITV depot, take a number, and wait nine hours to put your car through the hoops. You probably won't understand any of the instructions, most of which consist of utterances such as: "da-lay, da-lay, da-lay" (give it one, i.e. switch on the windscreen wipers, squirt the water spray, beep the horn etc.), tee-ra, tee-ra, tee-ra (keep going back), and "¡Para! (Stop!)". If all goes well, the car's *ficha técnica* (technical specifications card) will be stamped and you'll get a nice sticker for your windscreen. Otherwise, you have two months to get the vehicle into roadworthy condition. Driving without an up-to-date ITV will lose you four points off your licence under the new points system.

114

Jota J, the 11th letter of the Spanish alphabet. This is pronounced like the "h" in hot but more emphatically and with varying amounts of gravel in the throat: from a straightforward "huh" to a raspy "gghhuh".

Jaleo (gghhaLAYo) Din, uproar, muddle, row. An essential part of Spanish life.

JAMON
HURRY WHILE
STOCKS LAST!

Jamón Even vegetarians have been known to make an exception for premium-quality serrano ham, the kind that's cured from contented acorn-eating pigs who have lived their lives frolicking in the sierras. Theresa's Spanish friends can just about accept that she doesn't eat meat, but jamón? That's not meat, they say, that's jamón! Savoured and raved about all year long, the hallowed ham really comes into its own at Christmas.

One false turn in Carrefour and you end up trapped in a greasy sea of swinging forelegs and hind legs. Buy one, along with the special slender knife and the cutting stand that looks like an instrument of torture, and you are half-way to becoming Spanish. If you actually manage to mount the thing without losing a finger AND you master the fine art of sliver-slicing (thick chunks will NOT do), you can start applying for Spanish nationality.

Jamón/Jamona Back in the early 90s, we went to see a film directed by Bigas Luna called *Jamón, Jamón* (in which, incidentally, Penélope Cruz made her screen debut). It was years before we realised what the ham was all about: a bit of all right, a nice bit of trouser/skirt/crumpet, or indeed, for the more visceral Spaniards, a nice leg of ham. *"Eres un jamón/jamona"* might not do it for you, but it's up there with the choicest of comparable compliments like *"Estás como una moto* (You are like a motorbike)" or *"Estás como un tren* (You are like a train)." Whoever dreamed up the latter has obviously never travelled by rail in the UK...

Joder (hoDARE) F***. Very satisfying swear word due to the guttural gghh sound. Obviously not polite, yet depending on intonation often used in a mild knock-me-down-with-a-feather sort of way. Sometimes you may hear *"¡Jolines!"* (hoLEEEnes), a euphemism for *joder*.

K The letter k, pronounced "ka" (as in cat) is very seldom used in Castilian: almost all the words that have a k are of foreign origin, for example, words beginning with *kilo* such as *kilogramo, kilómetro, karaoke, kéfir, keynesiano.* But unofficially k is becoming more and more prevalent in words with a contracultural, street or punk context. It started in the 1980s with the *okupa* (squatter) movement, to differentiate from the "ordinary" meaning of *ocupar* (common or garden "occupy" as opposed to "squat"). K is now coming into its own to replace "qu" in email, Messenger, txt msgs (sorry, we've caught the bug too — we mean text messages), where of course *la ley del mínimo esfuerzo* (the law of least effort) holds sway. As in *¿a k hora kdamos? (¿a qué hora quedamos?). T kiero (te quiero).*

Kilo Apart from meaning 1000 grams, *un kilo* is still used to mean one million pesetas (6000 euros). We're used to handling everyday stuff in euros, but the really huge amounts are still not truly meaningful to many people — unless we're involved in football signings or major embezzlements on a daily basis. So we still tend to use *el kilo* as our point of reference. "250,000 euros for a dark, one-bedroom, no-lift hole in a back alley? That's over 40 KILOS! Whatever is the world coming to!"

La L **L-plate** (pronounced EH-lay). White on a green background. Bizarrely, you are allowed the honour of driving with the beep-at-me-I'm-an-idiot sticker only when you have passed your test, not before. As there is no such thing as a provisional licence, you may only, legally and expensively, learn to drive with a qualified instructor. The L-plate stays on your rear windscreen for one year, during which time you may not drive faster than 80kmh (a limit nobody would dream of exceeding). Theresa felt protected and excused with her EH-lay, especially when stuck in the slow lane behind a lorry/mounting the kerb/backing into a pillar/failing to parallel park in a space large enough for a fire engine/ever so slightly running over a pedestrian's foot at a zebra crossing. (Actually she did that last one on the second of eight attempts at passing her test). Now she's got no excuse. Apparently, 18 per cent of all accidents are caused by drivers in their first year.

Lampista In Catalonia the *lampista* vies with the *mecánico* and the *informático* for the title of everyone's most wanted. A *fontanero* (plumber) and *electricista* (electrician) rolled into one, he or she may also be a licensed gas fitter and fix telephone cables and sockets and sundry installations. This word has not yet become official in the Spanish language, but the trade/job description of *lampista* and the relevant training is to be introduced in the rest of Spain.

Leche You don't get milkmen in Spain, and neither, as a rule, do you get fresh milk. It's true that, if you rummage around in supermarket fridges near the orange juice and the butter, you'll probably find a few cartons; however, the vast bulk of the *leche*

119

consumed and sold is UHT, long-life. You may turn your nose up, but in the end you get used to it. Soya milk (*leche de soja*) is now sold by most supermarkets, though it is often relegated to the *dietética* (gluten-free, lactose-free, sugar-free, whatever-tastes-nice-free) section.

Anything to do with your mother (maternal milk in this case) or symbols of *macho*-ness (*leche* is also a vulgar term for semen) features heavily in colourful everyday expressions. Thus we have the Spanish equivalent of "bloody hell" with *me cago en la leche* (I crap in the milk), *tener mala leche* (lit. to have bad milk, to be full of nastiness or in a bad mood), *ser la leche* (to be a right little sod) and *irse cagando leches* (run off crapping milk, i.e. to clear off in a hurry, scarper).

Lehendakari Utterly unlike any other word for a leader or president or first citizen, this is the title given to the president of the Basque autonomous government. It sounds rather ancient and mysterious, but in fact was coined by the 19th-century nationalist Sabino Arana who derived it from *lehen* meaning first. He coined a host of new words, but *lehendakari* is one of the few that has found a permanent place in the Basque language.

Lepe So there's this guy from Lepe sitting in the village square throwing watches on the ground. Another guy from Lepe comes up and asks him what he's doing, and the first man says: "Killing time." Every country has jokes that portray people from a particular region as being seriously stupid — Spain has Lepe. We have to admit that we didn't realise until we did the research for this book that Lepe was a real place. But yes, it's a town in the province of Huelva, 41 kilometres from Huelva city, and in addition to the jokes, is Spain's strawberry capital. So anyway, one day three men, from Catalonia, Madrid and Lepe, are put through the lie detector. The Catalan says: "I think we

Catalans aren't as mean as we're made out to be." The machine bleeps. The Madrid fellow says "I think we *madrileños* aren't as cocky as people make out." The machine bleeps. The guy from Lepe says "I think..." The machine bleeps.

Libreta Bank book, and by extension, bank account. In the undignified scrabble for suckers, oops, we mean clients, banks and **cajas** have invented come-ons like the *libreta total* and the *libretón* (sort of big, whopping *libreta*), but don't forget that the Dalí tea sets and other junk mean only one thing: pathetic interest rates. When Valerie's financially-less-than-savvy father-in-law deposited several million pesetas in some *libreta* or other, he was given a pile of stuff: coffee machine, iron, toaster, radio alarm, electric knife. None of it ever worked.

Ll From 1803 to 1994 "ll" (pronounced more or less as "el-ye") was treated as a separate letter of the alphabet in the dictionary of the **Real Academia**. It still represents a separate sound (as in *calle,* Sevilla, *paella, llamar*) which is pronounced like an l but with the central part of the tongue humped up against the centre of the palate (linguists call it a palatal l). Can't manage it? Not to worry: neither can most Spanish speakers. While upheld as the standard by the **Real Academia**, the palatal l sound is notoriously unstable, with pronunciation varying from one country and region to another, from y (yamar), to j (jamar) to zh or sh (shamar). The "ll" is also a letter/sound in its own right in Catalan, characteristically at the beginning of words as in *llet (leche),* Llafranch (where Tom Sharpe lives) or the double whammy Ramón Llull, the famous 13th-century philosopher from Mallorca.

Llave inglesa The English key. None the wiser? Like the French kiss, Spanish fly and Dutch courage, *la llave inglesa* is a mystery to the nationality in question. It is, in fact, that supremely useful tool the monkey wrench.

121

Madrid It took three months for a copy of Valerie's marriage certificate, urgently needed, to come from Madrid. "If it were us, you'd have it in a couple of days," sniffed the **funcionarias** at the Barcelona Registry Office. "But... Madrid is Madrid." Poor Madrid. Let's face it, in Catalonia and other "peripheral" communities, the natives take a dim view: Madrid is a hotbed of high-handed centralists, a city of lazy, bar-lounging bureaucrats living off the fat of the rest of Spain. Madrid is a Black Hole into which our papers are sucked, never to re-emerge. So when Robert discovered he had to send his **bachillerato** and university entrance papers to some ministry or other in Madrid for legalisation so that he could enrol at a foreign university, he resigned himself to a second gap year, this one enforced. To his and Valerie's surprise and joy, they came back with their apostilles in only two weeks.

123

Of course, part of us knows that Madrid is a super-cool, got-its-act-together capital, cultured, cosmopolitan, dynamic, stylish, heritage-rich, packed with art, architecture, fabulous night life, bla, bla, bla, and that *madrileños* are human just like everyone else. But the spectre of pre-autonomy Spain, when everything had to be sorted in Madrid, still lurks in the collective unconscious. And, despite a pioneering degree of home rule, there are still things that have to be done in the capital. Valerie remembers once when Enric went to the Tribunal Supremo (Supreme Court) on a case. "How did it go?" she asked him when he got back. He grinned. "No problem. We sorted it all out with the judge. In the bar opposite. El Bar El Supremo." So Valerie asked Eduard what to write about Madrid. "If Spain were a doughnut," he said sagely. "Madrid would not exist."Quite.

(124)

Madrugada Considering that the Spanish are so fond of partying until the early hours, it is only right that they have a special word to describe them: *la madrugada*. "*Son las tres de la madrugada*" means it's three o'clock in the morning. Just to confuse things, *madrugada* also means daybreak and the verb, *madrugar,* means to get up at the crack of dawn. As in the children's goodnight ditty: "*Vamos a la cama, que hay que descansar, para que mañana podamos madrugar.* (Let's go to bed, we have to rest, so that tomorrow we can rise, bright and early)."

Mañana Morning, of course, but not as we know it (or used to know it). *La mañana* stretches until Spanish *mediodía* (midday), in other words until around 3pm, or at least until businesses knock off for lunch and kids finish school, around 2-2.30pm. The correct greeting during the extended morning is "*Buenos días*".

Manteca de cerdo While it is olive oil that is most readily associated with Spanish cuisine, *manteca de cerdo* (lard, literally pig butter) is a key ingredient in some of the most popular goodies, like *ensaimada* from Mallorca, one of Spain's **D.O.P.** products. *Ensaimada* dough is made with flour, water and *saim*, the Mallorcan word for lard.

Manteca de cerdo is sometimes used along with olive oil to start off roasts. In these days of "lite" cooking, it may be frowned upon, but it does give a characteristic flavour, along with garlic, herbs and brandy. Spaniards wouldn't dream of deep-frying in lard, however. *Manteca* is also a key ingredient of special treats we gorge on at Christmas: *polvorones*, incredibly short little cakes which melt in the mouth, not into crumbs but dust (*polvo),* and *mantecados*, flavoured with cinammon, aniseed, lemon or sweet wine. With sweets like these, who cares about cholesterol?

Marcha One of the first words Theresa learned in Spain, back when she had a lot of it, *marcha* that is. A city with *mucha marcha* is lively, has a great nightlife, while a person with it has lots of energy, is really into partying/having a good time as in *"Theresa tiene mucha marcha."* Could they really have said that about her? *Ir de marcha* means to go out on the town/paint the town red/go dancing till breakfast.

Martes y trece We all know that Friday the 13th is the day of death, doom and destruction. We've all endured at least trailers of the film, and besides we know that Jesus was crucified on a Friday and that 13 is universally unlucky (12 apostles plus a doomed Christ, and in Nordic mythology 12 gods plus a doomed Balder). In Spain, however, it is Tuesday 13, rather than Friday 13, that is deemed the dodgiest day of the year — supposedly because *martes* is named after Mars, the God of war and destruction. Nobody really believes in such nonsense.

Nonetheless, on this day, you're sure to receive lots of warnings. Mostly about marrying, such as: *"Martes y trece, ni te cases ni embarques/ni hijo cases, ni cochino mates/ni gallina eches ni hija cases* (Tuesday 13, don't get married or set off on a journey/ don't marry a son or kill a pig/don't put a chicken to mate or marry a daughter)."

Maruja Maruja, the name, is a diminutive of María. A *maruja*, however, is what the **Real Academia** calls a "housewife with a low level of culture". Derogatory? You bet. Sexist? Absolutely. A *maruja*, it's implied, is mainly concerned with gossiping, watching TV soaps and chat shows, and reading magazines like *Diez Minutos* and *Lecturas. Maruja.com* was an Internet-made-easy book published in 2000 for, surprise, *marujas*. The computer is not just for hubbies and kids, it warbled. It's a new all-purpose domestic appliance: find exotic recipes, look up what's on the telly, shop around the world. Patronising? The following year saw the release of a black comedy about two women who plotted to murder their husbands (one of them actually pulled it off). It was based on a true story. The title? *Marujas Asesinas*.

Matrícula Your car number plate. Also university fees, and the signing-up fee for all kinds of courses. When Theresa started teaching English some 15 years ago, all language schools tagged on a small *matrícula* to the monthly course fee. But nowadays, whether due to competition or capitulation in the face of protesting students and parents of students, the *matrícula* seems to be on the way out. Not so at the *autoescuelas* (driving schools), where you must cough up a hefty 100 euros plus to even step through the door.

Merienda Afternoon snack, eaten around the same time as the UK microwaves its dinner, in other words anytime between 5.30 and 7.00pm. Quite understandable, and necessary, if dinner's not until ten o'clock. Francisco, like many Spaniards, cannot do without his *merienda*. Wherever he and Theresa are in the world — in the Moroccan desert, on a remote beach in India, or at Theresa's parents' house in a small Midlands village, no matter what time they've had lunch and what time they're having dinner — room must be made for "afternoon snack". This typically consists of coffee and a filled roll, **churros**, a pastry or a slice of gooey cake.

Molar A young people's slang word, oft heard from the Spanish-dubbed Bart Simpson, meaning to be cool or hot, to rock, or the latest expression of approval. *"¡Este coche mola!"* conveys the idea that the vehicle in question is really something, it's great, it's fantastic. *"Esto no me mola"* really means "I don't like this" (it sucks). Like many other Spanish slang words (most of which have also been incorporated into Catalan unchanged) *molar* is originally from **caló**, the language of Spanish gypsies.

Moro Like the English "Moor", *moro* comes from the Latin "maurus", and was the name given to the inhabitants of Mauritania. When the Muslims invaded the Iberian Peninsula in the eighth century, the *moros* were just one part of the occupying forces, but gradually the term came to mean Muslims in general. Other than in a historical context, *moro* carries negative connotations and, like *sudaca* (South American) is best avoided. Although many people claim to use the word without malice, they should ponder the definition we spotted on a rather unpleasant online dictionary of Spanish slang: "Moro: A racist term applied to Muslim people (especially from Morocco) to show we don't want them here." Intention is all. *Bajarse al moro* was the title of a play by José Luis Alonso (1985) and later a film directed by Fernando Colomo (starring Veronica Forqué and Antonio Banderas) about a young couple who smuggle hashish into Spain. While the original meaning of *bajarse al moro* is to take a drug-smuggling trip south, these days it simply means to travel to Morocco.

127

Moros en la Costa *"No hay moros en la costa"* is the Spanish equivalent of the English expression "the coast is clear". It originated in the days when Berber pirates made frequent incursions along the Andalusia, Murcia and Valencia coasts. To protect themselves, those who lived close by built a series of watch towers. When the sentry on duty spied the pirates' sails in the distance, he would cry: *"¡Hay moros en la costa!"*, bells would be rung, and the townsfolk would prepare for the attack. From there, the expression came to be used to warn someone of impending danger.

Mossos d'Esquadra The "squad boys" is the historical and rather quaint name of the Catalan police force (*policía autonómica* or *policía de la Generalitat*). The boys (and girls) in navy with red trim trace their history back to the 18th century, which makes them the oldest police force in Spain. "What squad?" you may be asking. In 1714 the War of the Spanish Succession ended with the fall of Barcelona to Philip V, who was recognised as King of Spain, thus founding the Spanish branch of the Bourbon dynasty. Resistance simmered in occupied Catalonia which, in a bid for freedom, had backed the losing side. In 1719 nationalist guerrillas attacked the Bourbon-loyal city of Valls, but were repelled thanks to squadrons of armed civilians commanded by deputy mayor Pere Anton Veciana. In 1723 Catalonia's civilian squadrons were unified under Veciana, becoming an embryonic police force. The *Mossos* appeared and disappeared at various times in the 20th century, being crushed by Franco and reinstated when democracy returned. They have gradually taken over the functions of the Policía Nacional, and of the **Guardia Civil** in rural areas.

Movida, La Especially: **La Movida Madrileña**. The going on, the happening, Spain's equivalent of the Swinging Sixties. Term used to describe the hedonistic and cultural explosion of the 1980s, especially in music and the arts, following 36 years of dictatorship (Franco died in 1975, but the pent-up expression of Spanish youth really blew its cork after the PSOE Socialist Party won the elections in 1982). These were the days when Pedro Almodóvar worked for Telefónica, sang (we use the word loosely) in a semi-punk group, and at weekends directed his first full-length feature film *Pepi, Luci, Bom y Otras Chicas del Montón*. "Ay, *la movida*," sighs Francisco, recalling his misspent youth. "When we'd hitch-hike to Madrid (from Girona, around 700 kilometres away), party all night and then hitch back again." Used now to mean hassle, as in *"Hay mucha movida"*, there is a lot of hassle, for example, in buying a house.

Multa Fine. Most parking fines go straight from the windscreen into the nearest bin. Theoretically you pay them at the bank, and if you pay within 10 days you actually get a discount. Theresa stopped shelling out (ever so occasionally, you understand) when the teller rolled her eyes in a why-are-you-wasting-my-time-and-your money kind of way and said: "But nobody pays these!" In Spanish they "put" you a fine (*poner una multa*), rather than give you one.

Municipio The smallest administrative divisions of Spain, and the ones closest to the people, are the *municipios* (municipalities). Spain has 8108 *municipios*, according to the 2001 census. They are governed by elected municipal councils *(ayuntamientos)* and have executive powers for services such as transport, social services, sanitation and traffic. Their responsibilities vary according to the size of their populations. A *municipio* may be a village, town or city, or a country district. Aiguamúrcia in Tarragona province, for example, comprises seven villages including Aiguamúrcia proper, from which it takes its name, and Santes Creus, where the famous Cistercian monastery is located.

Mutua The everyday word for a private insurance company, from *mutualidad,* that is, mutual society. Large numbers of Spaniards, in particular **autónomos** (self-employed) have health care policies with these non-profit organisations, some of which also offer schemes for sick pay, invalidity benefit and so on. The big *mutuas* function almost like a parallel social security. Asistencia Sanitaria Colegial, for example, has its own hospital in Barcelona (a cooperative). It is definitely worth signing up for a *mutua,* especially if you live in a big city, where the social security services tend to be overloaded. When Eduard put his hand through a glass door, Valerie rushed him to **Urgencias** at Barcelona's nearest big public hospital, where they hit a four-hour queue. Off they rushed again, this time to the *mutua'*s own hospital, where Eduard was seen almost straightaway. Quotas are 60+ euros a month, depending on the plan you sign up for, and you get an electronic card to pay for doctor visits, tests and treatments. *Mutua* bureaucracy is fairly streamlined, but you still need to be very clear indeed about what is and isn't covered by your policy and how exactly to obtain it.

Naturismo Spain has more than 30 naturist camp-sites and resorts, including the four-star Vera Playa Club hotel in Almería and El Fonoll naturist village in Tarragona. Add to these more than 400 official naturist beaches and many more unofficial ones, and it's easy to see why Spain is fast becoming the number one tourist destination for those seeking an all-over tan. Attitudes to naturism are surprisingly relaxed, especially considering that the 60s (and half of the 70s) passed the country by — it was under the censorship and "morality"of a right-wing dictatorship. On many clothing-optional beaches you will see groups of families and friends, some starkers, some topless and others in swimsuits, all quite happily doing their own thing. The "freedom of image" and the right to dress (or not dress) as you see fit is enshrined in the Spanish Constitution, and theoretically you are allowed to be naked on any beach, or indeed in any public place. Walk down the high street *"en bolas"* (er, in balls), however, and you will probably be "invited" by the **Guardia Civil** to put your clothes back on.

In the 1920s and 1930s, as in Germany and the UK, Spain had a strong naturist movement, particularly in Catalonia. A number of magazines were published and nudist camps set up, with the emphasis being on healthy living, natural medicine and vegetarianism. The Civil War (1936-1939) put the wraps back on Spanish naturism, until Franco died in 1975. In 1979 the first two naturist resorts opened: Costa Natura, near Estepona on the Costa del Sol, and El Portús, near Cartagena in Murcia.

Nervioso Theresa never knew she was until she came to Spain. After just two private classes, her first language teacher declared she was *muy nerviosa*. Theresa couldn't understand — she's not a cautious, nervous sort of person at all. It took years for the meaning to become apparent. What the teacher wanted to say was that Theresa is the opposite of calm and relaxed. She's excitable, impatient and gets rattled easily. When she started teaching children she soon found out that most of them were extremely *nerviosos,* ie restless and unable to sit still for more than a nano-second.

NIF Número de Identificación Fiscal. See **CIF**.

Noche Evening/night. Starts at the end of the working/business day, around 8.30pm. Unlike "Goodnight", you say *"Buenas noches"* when you meet somebody at this time or go into a place, and not just when you are going to bed.

Nómina Payroll, payslip, salary, wages. One of the keys to personhood. Once you have a proper job and are *en nómina* (on the payroll) you're in the system. Way to go! Now you're eligible for all the free junk offered by your bank where you get your *nómina* paid in (*domiciliar la nómina*). If you don't have a *nómina* because you are self-employed, then you'll have to prove that you actually have some earnings by presenting income tax and VAT returns.

Notaría (NottaREEYa) Office of a **notario**.

Notario It often seems as if the whole of Spain spends half its time going to the notary. Valerie has never been to a *firma* (document signing) where she has not had to wait, sometimes for hours, among crowds of people. The notary finally zooms in, checks your ID and reads the document aloud at breakneck speed (theoretically they're supposed to make sure everyone understands what they're signing). It's all too tempting to mutter under your breath about cushy jobs, charging a fortune just to sit around scrawling your name with a flourish on official-looking papers, but in fact the notary (or his/her staff) has to go over all documents with a fine-tooth comb, making sure everything is in order. For example, in the case of a property sale, they have to check that the seller has no debts with the owners' association and verify all the details with the Property Register. If any discrepancy is found, then the signing will not go ahead. In Valerie's mind the word *notario* always used to conjure up the picture of an elderly, distinguished-looking gentleman in a pinstripe suit, so she was taken aback once by a *notaria* with dyed blonde hair, lots of gold earrings and bangles and necklaces, tight white jeans, high heels, and a black leather jacket covered in buckles, zips and studs that would have been the envy of any heavy metal fan.

Número Just make sure you get one. Some places have one or several number machines, others have receptionists who scribble them on bits of paper. At places like big council offices or the Seguridad Social, you may need human help just to figure out which option to punch on the high-tech *número* generator. Once Valerie was told by the receptionist at the health centre that she didn't need a *número* in order just to slip in and hand a paper to the nurse for the doctor to sign. She waited for half an hour, but the nurse (we guess it's not politically correct to say bloody-minded old battleaxe) refused even to look at her let alone take her paper, so she had to go back to reception and beg for a *número* and wait all over again. While theoretically having a *número* means that there should be no fighting, bitter hostilities may break out because there are different sets of *números*, and maybe no. 43 for repeat prescriptions is called BEFORE no. 5 for, say, the neurologist. We have even witnessed fights at the health centre about places in the before-lunch queue to get *números* assigned for the afternoon surgery. If there are no *números*, for example, at the bakery or the fishmonger's, find out who's last by shouting

"¿Quién es el último?" at the milling crowd (*"la última"* for all-female throngs) and stick like a limpet to whoever responds.

Ñ The 17th letter of the Spanish alphabet. Pronounced "enye". Originally the ñ developed from a double n, which scribes in the Middle Ages improvised to represent the new "ny" sound that had developed in the spoken language. Eventually, they opted for dropping a wiggly line (tilde) on top of a single n. Thus, sennor became **señor** and sennora, **señora**. Our old Simon & Schuster (bilingual) dictionary has just 44 entries for words beginning with the letter, the most difficult of which to pronounce is *ñoño* or *ñoña*, meaning dimwit or stupid. In Catalan the sound is written the way we would write it in English, as the digraph "ny". Hence, **Catalunya** (in Catalan), not Cataluña (in Castilian).

But "ñ" is not just a funny letter with a squiggle on top, it's a cultural icon, as Spanish as *paella*, Rioja, Don Quixote and especially *mañana* (manyana, *por favor*). In the 90s the EU kicked up a fuss over Spain's insistence that all imported keyboards come with the ñ in its rightful place next to the l and below the p. But the Spanish kicked up an even greater fuss and won the battle. How dare an EU directive question the inclusion of a letter that **España** needed to spell its own name? If you don't have a Spanish keyboard, you can insert the ñ from "symbols" in your WP programme, or do horribly complicated things with the keyboard configuration.

134

Ojalá I wish, if only. From the Arabic *"law sh'aa Allah"* (if God were willing).

ONCE (ONthay) The ONCE lottery booths are a characteristic feature of every Spanish town. In fact the Organización Nacional de Ciegos Españoles, the Spanish Blind People's Organisation, is one of the world's most powerful and influential associations for the blind and visually impaired. This public corporation was founded in 1938 to educate and provide employment for the blind, and was granted the lottery concession by the Spanish state. Sales of the *cupón* (lottery ticket) are its main source of revenue, financing a full range of services and facilities for the visually impaired, and, through the Fundación ONCE, for people with other disabilities. Since 2000 the ONCE has created 24,000 jobs for the disabled.

135

ONG Organización No Gubernamental. It's difficult not to call the Spanish equivalent of the NGO an-alien-from-a-sci-fi-movie, Ong, rather than an Oh ennay GGHAY.

Oposiciones *"Un trabajo para toda la vida* (a job for life)" is the catchline of a website for *opositores,* that is candidates for the *oposiciones*, the public competitive exams you must pass to obtain any kind of never-get-the-sack government job (national, municipal, or autonomic). And we're not just talking high-level civil servants, judges, notaries, university professors, tax inspectors and so on, or even the primary or secondary teachers' corps. For whether you dream of being an usher at the Spanish parliament, telephonist for the Basque health service, forest ranger for the government of Extremadura, or cleaner for Gran Canaria's island council, you have to memorise huge chunks of stuff, with the Spanish Constitution for starters. Fortunately, Spain is packed with *oposición* training academies. And you need them. To give one example: "distribution personnel" (aka postmen/women) for **Correos** have to master all sorts of laws and regulations and "an in-depth analysis of the postal sector within the European framework". The relevant text book (542 pages) will set you back 34 euros, 70 if you also want the mock exam papers and self-tests.

Ostras Oysters. And a euphemistic exclamation to avoid uttering that most terrible of Spanish swearwords: *hostia* (silent h), the host, or communion wafer. Used to express surprise, disgust, annoyance, etc.

PADRE This was going too far, we thought. How could they have the cheek to call the tax declaration form El Padre? We've already had to stomach the advertising campaigns designed to give **Hacienda** a more caring, friendly, helpful image. But The Father? We guess it wouldn't do much for their image to be honest and call it Big Brother. But it turns out that — how natty and clever — El Padre is the acronym of El Programa de Ayuda de la Renta (income tax return help computer program). It's updated every year and you can get it on CD or download it (*descargar el Padre*). It's said to be user-friendly and intuitive, and it even gives you your own bar code and saves you the hassle when you realise you've run out of your personalised labels on the last day for handing in your tax return. Lucky Valerie always gets her **renta** done at Enric's law office. She finds it stressful enough to get all the right papers together, but then the tax lawyer feeds the figures into El Padre, clicks the mouse a couple of times, and out pops the *renta*, ready to take to the bank. The only thing El Padre doesn't do, though, is actually pay your tax for you.

137

País Vasco Official Castilian name of the Basque autonomous community, but the term is also used more broadly by many to refer to the seven territories in which Basque is spoken: the provinces of Vizcaya, Guipúzcoa, Álava and Navarra in Spain, and Lapurdi, Low Navarre and Zuberoa in south-western France (part of the Pyrénées Atlantiques department). In this sense, it corresponds to *Euskal Herria* (Basque land or people).

Paleta In Catalonia this word (meaning small spade or trowel) refers to one of the most sought-after and at the same time dreaded individuals. *El paleta* is an *albañil*, the bricklayer/builder/workman who treads plaster into your carpet, puts a pickaxe through a water pipe and floods the downstairs neighbour, throws cigarette butts in your loo. No, that's not fair. The *paletas* Valerie had for her recent kitchen and bathroom renovation were a totally comic duo, consisting of a tall blond Romanian and short dark Colombian. They spent the entire day bickering and insulting each other and they did have the radio on horribly loud and she did find bits of mouldy sandwiches lying around. But she has to say they did a really great job. I.In other parts of Spain if somebody calls you *un paleto*, they don't think you lay bricks — they're branding you a yokel or country bumpkin.

Papa Your own daddy, or the daddy of the Catholic church. The Pope: El Papa.

Papeles Besides referring to papers in general, pre-euro slang for 1000-peseta notes.

Parking It may look and sound like an English word, but it has been seriously hijacked and refers not to the action of squeezing your vehicle into a vacant space, but rather to the space into which you squeeze it. In other words, *un parking* is a parking space or a car park. Of course, you can leave your car in a good old Spanish *aparcamiento* or *estacionamiento,* although this will require the utterance of several more syllables.

Paro/cobrar el paro Dole/to be on the dole. Vastly different to the UK system. You are granted *desempleo* (unemployment benefit), depending on the length of time you have worked. For example, if you have completed a year's contract and the contract is not renewed you are entitled to four months of *paro*; if you have worked for two years, you are entitled to eight months of *paro*, for three years, 12 months, and so on.

For the first six months you get 70 per cent of your official earnings, and 60 per cent thereafter. You sign on once every three months. This involves standing in line at the employment office (**INEM**), showing your ID, handing over a "looking for work card", and being given a new card with the next signing date stamped on it. No-one asks you any questions, nor are you asked to show proof of your job-seeking efforts. In fact, during the brief procedure your presence is barely acknowledged. When your dole money runs out, you may be entitled to a basic monthly payment called *el subsidio*. Otherwise, tough. Imagine, however, that after two months *en el paro* you find a job and sign off. You work for another year and then sign on again. You are still only entitled to four months benefit and you lose the other two unclaimed months. Naturally, the system encourages people to stay unemployed until they have claimed all they can. Some years ago, one of Theresa's brothers-in-law left his job, split up with his wife, and backpacked around the world for a year. Instead of forfeiting his dole money, he gave his ID card to one of his brothers, who signed on for him effortlessly. Such tricks come easy to the Garcías (see **familia numerosa**), but the system is asking to be abused. On the other hand, because you cannot claim dole money indefinitely, and because the family is still expected to act as a financial safety net, there is nothing like the benefit culture that exists in the UK.

Paso de peatones Pedestrian crossing. He/she should be so lucky. Look right, look left, look right again, glare defiantly at any approaching car and step out.

Pataleo (derecho de) You've tried everything, battled laboriously through every channel, but no way — the government, the bureaucrats or **Telefónica** win. You're in a Catch-22, a total no-win situation. "*Sólo nos queda el derecho del pataleo,*" you mutter. It means "We are only left with the right to complain", but the dictionary translation doesn't do

140

justice to the highly graphic and utterly Hispanic image evoked by the expression. *Pataleo* is from *pata* (animal's leg, used humorously or affectionately for human legs) and means the action of stamping, like kids throwing a tantrum. And so, when chaining yourself to the railings at some ministry or head office (as irate victims have been known to do) proves futile and serially murdering civil servants or nuking "customer service" is not an option, you still have the inalienable right to throw a tantrum.

Payo A word used by *gitanos* (gypsies) to describe those who are not gypsies. Considered by some to be slightly pejorative. Also means someone from a small village, or a country bumpkin. In Catalan, *un paio* is simply a bloke or guy.

Peña The basic meaning of this word is circle, group, club, with connotations of small and local. *Una peña taurina* is a bullfighting club, *una peña folklórica* a folk club and the group of workmates you play the lottery with is also *la peña*. The fan club, a late-20th-century import, does not qualify as a *peña*; it is *un club de fans*. *Peña* comes into its own in the world of football. The *peña madridista de Santiago*, for example, is the Real Madrid supporters' club of Santiago, the *peña barcelonista de Londres* is the Barcelona supporters' club of London. In general, your *peña* is your gang, your group of friends. And in today's slang, *la peña* often just means people.

Persiana A blind. We had to make an effort to remember that. Those of us who have been here a long time invariably find ourselves mystifying visitors by talking about persian blinds or even persians. The person who fixes *persianas* is the *persianero*. Like plumbers, glaziers and locksmiths, *persianeros* have emergency numbers and, naturally, will charge you a small fortune when you're on your balcony hanging out the washing or spying on the neighbours and the *persiana* cord snaps. Venetian blinds are, logically, *persianas venecianas*.

Pesetas/pelas The peseta (slang word *pela*), legal tender in Spain until the advent of the euro in 2002, is still an essential reference point for most of us, especially for ritual moaning about the Great Price Hike. As in: they're charging tourists nine euros for a beer on the Rambla. THAT'S 1500 PESETAS FOR GOD'S SAKE! Or: I had to pay 120 euros for this man to change a bit of rubber on my washing machine. THAT'S 20,000 PESETAS FOR GOD'S SAKE! In cash! For a bit of rubber! He was only here for five minutes! I didn't have enough cash so he marched me to the ATM on the corner at monkey-wrench point... And so on and so on and so on.

But of course the only really meaningful reference point is what things cost in relation to what you earn. Valerie's parsimonious (all right, mean) father-in-law had his own version of the Great Price Hike rant: "Before the war this cost one peseta." He would say it about more or less everything. But before the war, Valerie would point out, most people earned only a few pesetas a week.

Piñata Essential for kids' parties. The *piñata* is a cardboard container stuffed with sweets and lollipops which is hung from the ceiling (or wherever you can manage). The kids have to smash it with a stick (or umbrella) whereupon it falls apart and they get over-excited and roll around on the floor screaming and kicking and fighting over the contents. We think the original tradition requires this to be done blindfold (we mean the bashing with the stick), but this is clearly not a sensible idea.

142

Plazo/plaza Take heart. Between us we've been in Spain for nearly 50 years and we still can't get *plazo/plaza* right. It's so embarrassing, after all this time, to find ourselves asking the guy in the showroom how many town squares we would have to pay on a new car. But writing this book has led to the moment of truth — we must get our heads around it. In Spanish *plaza* is used as a catch-all. *Una plaza de parking* is a parking space in a garage, rented or owned, costs the earth. *Una plaza universitaria* is a university place. *Una plaza hotelera* is a hotel bed. *Una plaza de trabajo* is a job. *Una plaza* on a plane, train, ship etc is a seat. *Una plaza*, in this general, conceptual sense, is a piece of occupiable space.

Now it's all falling into place: *un plazo* relates not to space but to time — it's a portion of time with a limit, a sell-by date as it were. *¿Qué plazo tenemos?* we ask our translation clients. What's the deadline? What's the *plazo* for paying my VAT?

Un depósito a plazo fijo is a fixed-term deposit (don't do it: however many wondrous digital pressure cookers your bank is offering as a prize, interest is pathetic and your capital doesn't grow). *Pagar a plazos* means to pay in installments and the *plazo* is the installment or payment itself.

Pompas fúnebres This grandiloquent phrase does not refer to some kind of ceremonial funeral with marching brass bands, horse-drawn carriages and other stately paraphernalia. It is the blanket word for funeral services of any kind, funeral parlour, funeral director, undertaker, or funeral management in general. Normally in Spain funerals are held within 24 hours of death, but they can be delayed to allow for family or friends to arrive, in which case the body will be kept in a morgue at additional cost. Now here is an interesting nugget of information: Funespaña is the leading Spanish group specialising in full funeral service provision. It operates in five autonomous communities and has also gone multinational, having cracked the Hungarian market, where it is now number two. On a more practical note, for information in plain English about what to do if someone dies in Spain, there's an excellent factsheet at www.acespana.org/acespana/info_571.htm

Porfa Go on, *porfa*. Please, please. *Por favor*. Geddit?

Portero Another word for **conserje**: caretaker. Also the chap or chapess who stands in goal in a football match.

Prensa rosa The pink press. Nothing to do with flowers or gay publications. Everything to do with the glamorous lives, houses and holidays of peripheral aristocrats, bullfighters, top models, footballers who hang out with top models, sheiks on holiday in Marbella, *Operación Triunfo* (Pop Idol) winners, *Gran Hermano* victims, the royal families of Europe (especially the Monaco dynasty), down-at-heel celebrities, and anyone who has ever known/had a blazing row with/had a child by any of the former. *Hola, Diez Minutos, Lecturas, Pronto, Qué me dices*, the list of gossip magazines goes on. (We know all of this, of course, because we have to do something when we go to the hairdresser´s.). For true addicts, daytime and weekend evening television offers wall-to- wall "pink" programmes, where panels of "experts" sit around and analyse who's doing what with whom and why. The most famous of these is called *Salsa Rosa* (Pink Sauce).

Primera comunión First communion. A complete mystery to one who did not grow up in the Catholic faith (or any faith for that matter). At the age of eight or nine, children suddenly have to fit in *catequesis* classes with their 98,000 other extra-curricular activities. After learning the various what-Catholicism-is-all-about precepts off by heart, the child partakes of his or her first communion at a special mass (usually in May), receives hundreds of presents and has a whopping great party at a restaurant or hotel. During the last 10 years or so, first communions have spiralled out of all financial proportion, with the average family now spending over 3000 euros per child. The most expensive items are the clothes and accessories of the communee (girls in white meringue dress and boys in military uniform or sailor suit) and the wedding-style banquet, with typically 50-100 guests at 30-36 euros a head. You may think "I'm not Catholic, it won't affect my child". Wrong. No-one likes seeing their kids left out, and peer pressure is so strong at school ("But mum, everyone else gets loads of presents") that you will probably find yourself relenting.

Propina A tip. *Dejar una propina*: to leave a tip. So whom should you tip? And how much? Despite their generosity when it comes to buying drinks, paying for meals, giving presents, etc., the Spanish are not the greatest tippers in the world. When visitors come from the UK, they think we're being stingy when we tell them that five euros for a 50 euro meal is too much. But that's just the way it is; two or three would be plenty. On the other hand, it's definitely customary to leave your change in a bar after having a coffee or a snack. As for taxi drivers, hairdressers, and pizza deliverers, some people do and some people don't. Personally, if Theresa has change, she leaves it; and if not, not. Valerie always tips the petrol pump attendant on the rare occasion that the petrol station is not self-service. Theresa and Francisco don't. Perhaps because in their part of Malaga, most *gasolineras* are NOT self-service and, the piecemeal way they put petrol in their car, they wouldn't have any money left over actually to buy any if they tipped every time. One person you should definitely reward if you live up a flight or six of stairs is the **butanero**, the gas-bottle man.

Provincia If we read one more travel guide or feature that refers to Catalonia, Valencia or Andalusia (to name only the best-known) as provinces, we'll scream. As we will if we see one more website with a pretty coloured map of the **Comunidades Autónomas** that says "Click to select province". Comunidades Autónomas and provinces are not the same thing. Perhaps the confusion arises from the fact that seven of the autonomous communities are, indeed, composed of just one province. But huge Andalusia, for example, is formed by eight: Malaga, Granada, Sevilla, Córdoba, Jaén, Cádiz, Almería and Huelva. And each province has its provincial capital, often, but not always, with the same name.

Spain was officially divided into provinces in 1833, by royal decree, as part of a liberal revolution which laid the foundations for a new centralised state. This division is essentially still in place, the only major modification being the division of the Canary Islands into two provinces in 1927. Before the transfer of many of the state powers to the Comunidades Autónomas, all the ministries had delegations in the provincial capitals, still the case with **Tráfico** and **IMSERSO**. The provinces are used as electoral districts, in postal addresses and as geographical references. Phone area codes are provincial, and many professional associations and other organisations are province-wide.

Puente A bridge. But also a great anti-work-ethic institution, whereby if a public holiday falls on a Tuesday (or a Thursday), Monday (or Friday) is thrown in for good measure. The year is littered with *puentes*. They are the life-blood of travel agencies, which offer special deals for, among others, the *puente del Pilar* (Oct 12), the *puente de Mayo* (May 1), and best of all, the *puente de la Inmaculada/de la Constitución* (December 6 and December 8). When December 6 falls on a Tuesday and December 8 on a Thursday, it makes a mega triple *puente*. What with Christmas and New Year, December is about as productive a month as August (when everyone is on holiday and all bureaucratic procedures grind to a halt). Whether or not the *puente* will survive Spain's creeping Northern Europeanisation remains to be seen.

146

Puticlubs and putas Sounds so cute, like a Saturday morning cartoon show. In fact, *puti* comes from *puta,* meaning whore, and a *puticlub* is a bar-cum-brothel. Also known more euphemistically as *clubs de alterne* (hostess clubs), they are normally located out of town on quiet secondary roads, their tell-tale neon lights flashing like mini-Las Vegases. Regardless of what they say, most Spanish men have been to one, if only for a very expensive glass of coloured water. In the *macho* business world it is still customary to wind up an evening of wining and dining your clients with a trip to the local *puticlub.*

According to a survey by Spain's National Statistics Institute in 2003, over a quarter of Spanish men have paid for sex at least once in their lives. The trade union Comisiones Obreras estimates that of the 400,000 women working in the sex trade, 90 per cent are immigrants, mostly from Africa, South America and Eastern Europe. Prostitution is neither legal nor illegal; it is simply not covered by Spanish law. Over the last few years, unions, women's groups and prostitutes' collectives have called for changes in legislation which will recognise the rights of sex workers. In 2002 the Catalan government passed a law requiring brothels to be regulated. The present Socialist government in Madrid has promised to open a debate on the wider issue of prostitution and the law. Very large sparks are sure to fly.

PYME Pronounced PEEmay. Acronym for Pequeña y Mediana Empresa: small- and medium-sized firm (not to be confused with the long-life yogurt made by PMI, pronounced payemmayEE). Because the name sounds like something dreamed up for kids' TV and the BankPyme logo with three little stick-people is so cute, you may imagine *pymes* to be tiny family firms. But according to the definition given by the European Commission in May 2003, a *pyme* may have as many as 250 employees and an annual turnover of up to 50 million euros or an annual general balance of up to 43 million euros. These, it turns out, are the medium-sized ones. Small firms employ less than 50 people and have an annual turnover or balance of no more than 10 million euros. Fewer than 10 employees and a turnover of a paltry two million euros, and you're officially a *microempresa*.

Q Pronounced as in Koo Stark. The 19th letter in the Spanish alphabet.

Quedar The basic meaning is to stay or remain. We struggled for years with *citas* (dates and certain kinds of appointments) and **horas** (appointments but not dates) and assorted *reuniones* and *encuentros* until it clicked, after hearing it used thousands of times, that *quedar* also means "to arrange to meet". For example, *"He quedado a las 9 con Pepe"* means "I'm meeting Pepe at 9". *"He quedado"* (I'm meeting someone, or possibly something) is suitably vague and secretive and is therefore to be heard a great deal in Spanish TV soaps (followed by slamming door), provoking fits of suspicion and jealousy on screen and edge-of-seat suspense in the viewer.

Queimada The dictionary says "Hot Galician punch". Hmmm. Valerie's first experience of a *queimada* was, of all places, in Valencia: a seduction scenario set up for her and her friend by their student wannabee lovers from **Galicia**. God knows what the guys poured into it: the result was knock-you-out potent. Picture the scene. A darkened room. The mystery liquid is set alight, mesmerising blue fire plays around the earthenware dish, an expert hand slowly stirs with a ladle, making the flames leap. The potion is handed round in little earthenware bowls...the head spins... You would have been seduced, too, wouldn't you? The original *queimada* is made by burning *orujo* (*aguardiente*) with lemon and sugar. There seems to be considerable controversy about the recipe, though. While some people add a little coffee, ground or whole, and others add fruit, raisins, cinnamon, red wine or rum, purists admit only *aguardiente*, sugar (100 grams per litre of *aguardiente*), and

149

the zest of a perfectly ripe lemon. The fiery brew should be stirred without the ladle touching the bottom of the dish. The key is to know when to blow out the flames, which, like birthday candles, should be done with a single puff. The true essence of the *queimada*, which should really take place outdoors, is its ritual aspect: it's said to originate with the ancient Celts and to be related to the casting of an anti-witchcraft spell. The Catalan version of hot punch is called *cremat,* and is traditionally made with rum.

Quinqui False friend, not meaning kinky, but rather delinquent or petty thief. For a "real" kinky, you would use *pervertido*. Dig a little further, however, and you discover that *quinqui* is a contraction of *quinquillero* or *quincallero*, meaning metalsmith, and that the Quinquis are/were a semi-nomadic people who traditionally earned their living by selling cheap metal goods from door-to-door — rather like the Irish Travellers, or "Tinkers". Ignored by mainstream society and regarded as low-life, Quinquis were often blamed for petty crime; hence the evolution of the meaning of *quinqui* into hoodlum or thief. Owing to the pejorative overtones of the word, they prefer to be known as *mercheros*. Like the gypsies, the *mercheros* have their own dialect, *quinqui*, an old form of Castilian related to **caló** and Germania, but not Romany. Ethnologists are uncertain where they originally came from, but it is thought that they could be: a) of Central European origin, b) descended from landless peasants, c) descendants of Muslims who became nomads to escape persecution after their expulsion in 1610 by Phillip III, d) a mixed gypsy-**payo** (non-gypsy) race, or e) a mixture of all three.

During the 1950s the *mercheros* were forced by the Franco regime to quit their wandering ways and form permanent settlements, which they did, setting up sprawling slums on the edges of large cities. Their population today stands at an estimated 150,000, and the largest communities are in Valencia, Madrid, Bilbao and Catalonia.

Radares Speed cameras. Rapidly springing up all all over the place, as part of the government campaign to reduce the number of accidents on the road. If you're blind and miss the giant signs warning of cameras ahead, you'll soon realise you should slow down when suddenly you're leading all the other traffic.

Ratoncito Pérez Little mouse Pérez: the tooth mouse. There you are, in bed aged seven, you've lost a tooth and it hurts. But then the tears dry and you get all excited when you remember -- oh frabjous joy! -- that a small rodent will shortly be nuzzling by your ear and burrowing under your pillow. Ratón Pérez! Forget about sweet little fairies; in Spain (and France and Italy, and in South America) it's the tooth mouse that leaves you cash or goodies in return for your milk teeth. Sounds like something out of Disney, and in a way it is. Although the idea of a tooth mouse had been around for hundreds of years, it was Jesuit priest and writer Luis Coloma who brought the mythical creature to life in a short story he wrote in the 1890s, dedicating it to Alfonso XIII, then aged eight. (El rey Bubi, as the young king was affectionately known, had just lost a tooth, and Coloma actually made him the main character in the tale.) The short story was published in 1911 and from there the legend spread. Thanks to Coloma's story, all Spanish children know that Ratón Pérez wears gold glasses and a straw hat, carries a red satchel on his back, and lives with his family in a biscuit tin in a sweet shop at Calle Arenal, 8, in Madrid. There is even a plaque on the wall of the building (today, a shoe shop) to commemorate his "birthplace". In 2003 the cartoon series *Factoría Ratonil Pérez* was shown on Spanish television. And

151

while Disney didn't jump on the mouse-wagon, Spain's Filmax and Argentina's Patagonik did, with their 2006 co-production of *El Ratón Pérez*, a 3-D animated film, digitally integrated with real actors and settings.

At www.ratoncitoperez.com, a site dedicated to teaching children about dental care in a fun way, you can actually order a genuine silver coin engraved with your child's name for just (gulp) over 60 euros.

Real Academia Española *"Limpia, fija y da esplendor."* Cleans, fixes, and gives splendour. This is the motto not of a new all-powerful, dirt-annihilating detergent, but of the Royal Academy of the Spanish Language (RAE), founded in 1713, thirteen years before Castilian (see **castellano**) was declared to be the official language of Spain by Phillip V. As Spain's empire broke up, it was feared that Castilian would suffer the same fate as Latin and morph into lots of related but unintelligible languages. The aim of the Real Academia was thus to "fix the words and vocabularies of the Castilian language with propriety, elegance and purity" and ensure that the same rules of spelling and grammar would be applied all over the Spanish-speaking world. Based in Madrid, the organisation is affiliated to the royal academies of 21 other Spanish speaking nations, and is a major publisher of dictionaries and grammars, most notably the *Diccionario de la Real Academia Española (DRAE)*.

These days Real Academia bashing is almost *de rigueur* among journalists and writers (ourselves included), who accuse it of being conservative, elitist, centralist (giving undue emphasis to the Castilian as it is spoken and used in Madrid), out of touch, and sluggishly slow in accepting new spellings, words and usages. There is something that all schoolchildren and students of Spanish as a foreign language have to thank the academy for, however. In the early years, the RAE implemented hundreds of changes to make spelling represent pronunciation more closely, with the result that today Spanish is one of the easiest languages to transcribe in the world.

Receta médica Prescription. Not long-winded enough? How about *prescripción facultativa?* Social security prescriptions are quite cheap, and free for pensioners, people with disabilities, etc. It used to be easy to buy *medicamentos con receta* (prescription drugs) over the counter from your friendly, lax local **farmacia** but now they're tightening up. A *receta* is also a recipe, so the word harks back to the time when pharmacists actually made up medicines from diverse ingredients. Now, though, instead of mysterious poundings, mixings and shakings, they have been largely reduced to taking a bottle or packet from a shelf and wrapping it up. Unlike their counterparts in the UK, Spanish pharmacists don't even have to count out the exact number of pills prescribed by the doctor and put them in bottles. But they have evolved a new ritual around social security prescriptions; the perforated bit with the price and bar code is removed from the pack and attached to the *receta*, which is then filed. After waiting in long lines at numerous *farmacias* (Spanish doctors routinely overprescribe, by the way), we have yet to see two pharmacists do this in the same way. The combinations of scissors, cutters, knives and teeth, sellotape, paper clips, adhesives and staplers, and styles of cutting, sticking and putting in little piles appear to be infinite.

Recibo A receipt. What you get after you have paid a bill, right? But in Spain, you're more than likely to get your receipt *before* you pay the bill. In fact the *recibo is* the bill. In the old days, when *recibos* came through the post or people knocked on your door with them demanding cash, once you had paid up the *recibo* would be stamped and serve as the receipt. Now the whole thing has been cleverly streamlined via the *de rigueur* **domiciliación bancaria** for everything from gas and electricity

153

to yoga classes to the installments on your car. *Pagar un recibo* now means to pay a direct debit. *Un recibo* is also a receipt in all the usual senses. In shops, make sure you get one — usually called *el tíket* if it comes out of the cash register — which you will need in order to return the goods if they are faulty.

RENFE One of the few Spanish institutions whose initials form a pronounceable word: RENfay. Red Nacional de los Ferrocarriles Españoles: National Network of Spanish Railways. "La Renfe" was set up in 1941 when the great broad-gauge railway companies were put into state administration, with the priority aim of rebuilding the rail infrastructure badly damaged during the civil war. Renfe has finally reinvented itself as the transport of choice for the truly cool, and some of the newest trains look like they were just time-warped in from a sci-fi movie. The Renfe website is peopled with grinning *Baywatch* men dashing around with surfboards and shiny happy families with buckets and spades. The significance of this is lost if you never experienced how awful Spanish trains could be back in the 1970s and early 80s, before Renfe started getting its act together. The name Renfe can still conjure up rib-crunching crowds on Saturday morning *costa* trains, endless hours of cramped rattling and jolting, and unusable toilets. These days people rave about Renfe, but Valerie's Eduard and Robert believe they know what the acronym really stands for: *Rogamos Empujen Nuestros Ferrocarriles Estropeados* (Please push our broken-down railways).

Renta Not rent, which is **alquiler,** but income in general. It usually means unearned income (for example if you invest your money and live off the interest). However, for tax purposes it refers to all income from all sources, whether earned by working (*renta del trabajo personal)* or not. And you have to put all your official income (including the couple of cents of interest your bank has oh-so-generously awarded you) on your Declaración de la Renta (income tax return) or *la renta* as it is known. Do not attempt to do **gestiones** with **gestores** or lawyers in late June — it's *renta* time (deadline is June 30) and everyone will brush you off alleging they're up to their eyes *con las rentas*.

Residencia What we used to call the residence permit. *La residencia* is the everyday term for the foreigner's residence card, officially called *la tarjeta de extranjeros*, a credit-card sized ID with your photo, personal details and fingerprint. Applying for your *residencia* (there's comprehensive information in plain English on this at www.expatica.com Spain pages) may be one of the biggest bureaucratic hurdles you will face, and famously takes months and months. You need to renew your foreigner's card every five years — and if you lose it or it is stolen. Remember *burrocracia?* It took Theresa five trips to the *Comisaría* and a mere 15 months to get her card replaced. A staff shortage, they said.

Revisar, revisión Besides corresponding to the English "revise" and "revision" for things like prices, methods and doctrines, in Spanish it is used when talking about checking or check-ups or inspections. You can *revisar* (check or look through) a document, an expense account or a spreadsheet, for example, or *revisar la ortografía* (check the spelling) of a book or article. A *revisión médica* is a medical examination or check-up. A *revisión* of a machine or installation is an inspection or even an overhaul. A *revisión técnica* of a vehicle is a roadworthiness check. When you're revising for exams, though, you're not checking for mistakes or faults as in a *revisión*, but going over the material. This is *repasar.* Or just plain *estudiar* because you probably never studied the stuff the first time around.

Reyes Kings' Day, January 6. While the Three Kings traditionally bring the presents, the imported Papa Noel will already have done his bit for the toy manufacturers two weeks earlier. There

155

is still no way, however, that Santa can compete with the sheer spectacle and buzz of the Kings' *cabalgata* (cavalcade) that takes place on the evening of January 5 in every city, town and two-bit *pueblo*. The night belongs to the innocence of young children who watch spellbound as Melchior, Balthasar and Gaspar, decked in all their exotic finery, parade down the main drag on tractors, horses or even camels, gaudy thrones in tow, throwing sweets and toys behind them. Later, their majesties deliver the presents from balcony to porch to front door, stopping off for milk and biscuits (water for the camels). Presents are ripped open next morning, and one final Christmas feast follows.

RNE Radio Nacional Española. The state-owned broadcasting company kicked off in 1937 in the middle of the Civil War, providing Franco with a state-of-the-art propaganda weapon (Spain's first radio transmitter, a Telefunken, was actually a present from Nazi Germany to the new Fascist state). Although private stations sprang up after the war, RNE had complete control of all news reports, right up until 1977. When news time came, the stations switched through to the censored RNE broadcasts, after which listeners were browbeaten with the national anthem and the invocation: *Gloriosos caídos por Dios y por España. ¡Presentes!* (The glorious fallen for God and for Spain. Present in spirit!)

Today there are six RNE channels, the most popular and populist of which is Radio 1. Radio 5 offers 24-hour news and is broadcast worldwide. With more than 80 million people tuning in daily, only the BBC World Service and Radio Vatican have more listeners.

Rodríguez When school is out from late-June to mid-September and the towns and cities roast, traditionally wives and kids are evacuated to beach apartments, country villas, the in-laws' *pueblo*, while the men stay home to, er, work. This *macho* staying home alone is known as *quedarse de rodríguez*. Why *rodríguez*? So far we have been unable to find out. But his days may be numbered. Unfortunately for Spanish men, as more and more women work and holidays get shorter in line with northern Europe, the bliss of staying in town *en plan rodríguez* is increasingly confined to just the odd weekend.

Rollo Drag, bore, pain. *¡Qué rollo!* Quintessential expression for teenagers and moaners everywhere. Open your books at page 77. *¡Qué rollo!* Tidy your room. *¡Qué rollo!* I´ve bought you a round-the-world plane ticket. *¡Qué rollo!* What a drag! Something or someone that makes you feel uneasy or gives you the creeps is said to have *mal rollo* (bad vibes, man). Likewise, if someone has *buen rollo,* they give off good vibrations. On a more practical level, *un rollo de papel higiénico* is a toilet roll, *un rollo de película*, a roll of film, and *un rollo de cuerda*, a coil of rope.

157

Romería A horse-and-wagon pilgrimage into the countryside to visit the shrine of some miracle-producing Virgin or saint, followed by singing and dancing and feasting. Comes from *romero*, used to describe the pilgrims who traditionally walked to Rome. If you live in Spain, you should go on a *romería* at least once. Theresa's friend Joanna is not so sure. Due to new strict anti-forest-fire regulations, gone are the days of sitting around the camp fire after a hard day's ride/walk. Now it's more like shiver in your sleeping-bag and go home the next day tired, frozen and grumpy. At least that's what Joanna says. For the undeterred, the most famous — and biggest — of all the *romerías* is that of La Virgen del Rocío, which is celebrated the weekend before Whit Monday, near Almonte in the province of Huelva. Televised every year, the mega Catholic-cum-pagan bash attracts a staggering one million devoteees, with the participation of more than 100 brotherhoods and virtually the entire gypsy community of Andalusia. For the **gitanos** the *romería* is an emotionally charged back-to-one's-roots experience, and many make the pilgrimage from all over Spain and central Europe.

Apart from the sheer numbers, what makes El Rocío so spectacular is the fact that the Virgin's shrine is located in the middle of the marshlands of the Guadalquivir river delta (part of the Doñana National Park). To reach it, thousands of people, dressed up to the folkloric nines, accompanied by tambourines, drums, guitars and flutes, trek for several days across sand dunes and marshes, on foot and horseback, in carriages and four-wheel-drives. The pilgrimage reaches a near-hysterical climax when the Virgin's image is paraded around the Rocío hamlet to endless chants of *"¡Viva la Reina de la Marisma! ¡Viva!* (Long live the Queen of the Marshes)". Rocío has been the patron saint of Almonte since the 15th century when a hunter found a statue of the Virgin in a tree trunk in the marshes. Devotees claim that her powers can cure disease, infertiltity and mental disorders.

Roscón de Reyes Kings' Day Bun. "Mm, look what I've bought," says Francisco every January 5, thrusting under Theresa's nose a giant, ring-shaped bun with a few bits of red and green candied peel stuck on top and a plastic toy hidden somewhere inside for her to break a tooth on. She fails to show much enthusiasm. "But this one's got loads of cream in it," he raves. It's an improvement, she supposes, but it can't beat good old Christmas cake. In Catalonia, the traditional *tortell de reis* comes with a cardboard crown and contains a broad bean, *una fava*. The lucky (toothless) person who finds it is proclaimed Bean King and gets to wear the crown. And also has the royal duty of reimbursing whoever shelled out for the cake. Nowadays, the *tortell* also contains a bean-sized ceramic king, the finder of which is, logically, crowned king, while the *fava*-finder has to pay. Apparently, once upon a time Twelfth Night cakes were popular in England, too. Only they were rich and dark and thickly iced and contained a lucky pea as well as a bean.

RR Unlike the other two digraphs, **ll** and **ch**, rr (pronounced erre) is not considered a letter in its own right. Like the r in the initial position (*rosa, roca, receta*), it is pronounced with a rolling trill. That's the theory at any rate. In the early years, Theresa would pound the streets, a woman possessed, ranting her "erres" over and over again, like a growling dog with a speech impediment. *Perro, carretera, río, roca, arroz* — she ruined them all. She still can't trill to order, but ever so occasionally she gets all excited when a perfectly rolled "erre" slips out unbidden. To avoid sounding like a lisping English person (the Scottish have no problems and neither does Valerie), put the flap of your tongue against the roof of your mouth, think of cats purring, and hope for the best. And, if it helps, try visualising your tongue flapping around in a strong wind. Should you manage to get the hang of trilling, you can drive yourself crazy with this *trabalenguas*, or tongue twister:

> *Erre con erre cigarro*
> *Erre con erre barril*
> *Rápido corren los autos*
> *Por la vía del ferrocarril*

159

RTVE Radiotelevisión Española, the Spanish public broadcasting company that includes **TVE** (Televisión Española) and **RNE** (Radio Nacional de España).

While children still play *inocentadas* on this day all over Spain and South America, it is in Valencia where the old tradition of a period of temporary misrule best lives on in the fiesta of "Els Enfarinats" (the men with flour-caked faces). Once they've elected their mayor for the day (and a judge and a prosecutor), the flour-faced gang stirs up mock trouble around town, imposing fines, reading humorous edicts and criticising local dignitaries and institutions.

Sardana The Catalan national dance and one of the great symbols of Catalan culture, famously banned by Franco and danced at clandestine meetings in private houses. We know we'll probably get shot for saying this, but we find it hard to see what the fuss is about. The *sardana* is terribly sedate, and, given the intricate footwork, the dancers' faces are set in oh-so-serious, this-is-our-national-treasure concentration. The music, played by a *cobla* (a woodwind and brass band of 11 players) is, to our ears, repetitive and borderline irritating. But, as the Catalans point out, the *sardana* is totally democratic. Just throw your coat and bag on the heap in the centre and join the circle. You don't need to wear espadrilles, but it helps.

165

SEAT (Pronounced 'SAYat') We'd always known that SEAT was a Spanish version of Fiat, but we admit we have only just found out that it stands for Sociedad Española de Automóviles de Turismo (Spanish Private Car Corporation). Originally a joint initiative of the Spanish government and Fiat, it was founded in 1950 as a subsidiary of the Italian firm, with an important share owned by the Spanish government. Initially, SEAT manufactured rebadged Fiat models. Fiat withdrew in 1981 and the Volkswagen Group signed a cooperation agreement with SEAT, becoming the major shareholder in 1986, and owner of 100 per cent of the company in 1990. SEAT has its plant in Martorell (near Barcelona), where more than 450,000 cars are manufactured every year.

Segurata Slang word for security guard.

Seguridad Social If you feel pretty clueless about the Seguridad Social, you're in good company. Valerie's husband Enric always dealt with this stuff. Now she follows her **gestor's** instructions. "Is it me, or is this really incomprehensible?" she whines to him on the phone, as he talks her through an attempt to download the application forms for self-employed sickness benefit. She hears him tapping and clicking, and mumbling consolingly: he's got the stuff onscreen, they've changed it yet again, can't figure it out himself..."*en fin, es un lío* (It's a mess)". Later Valerie checks and double-checks with him about where to take the forms, armfuls of photocopies and rabbit's foot. That building on Calle Industria, the one she's been past loads of times on the 45 bus? NO, that's Tesorería. You want the INSS (pronounced "eens"). She finally gets it, more or less. Very basically, the Instituto Nacional de la Seguridad Social deals with benefits (except unemployment), and it's where you get your European Health Card. The Tesorería General de la Seguridad Social (TGSS) manages the financial resources of the social security system and is where all companies in Spain and their employees have to be registered. It also controls the employers and employees' social security contributions.

So what happened at the INSS? Valerie's **número** was called (we should say flashed on the screen to the sound of bells and whistles) almost straight away, and the **funcionaria** was pleasant and businesslike. But you can never defy the One Thing Missing Law of Spanish Bureaucracy. It turned out that the doctor had got the dates on Valerie's sick note wrong. And yes, she had to drag herself back to the health centre, get a **número**, wait for hours on a plastic chair, etc. etc. Be warned.

Seguro Insurance policy, safety catch, clasp, fastener. *El seguro* refers to the state health care system as in *"Me operé por el* seguro (I had my op on the National Health)". The alternatives are *por la mutua* (on private mutual society insurance), or *particular* (privately).

Seiscientos Way back in 1968, Valerie experienced her first ride in the car of an ordinary Spaniard, one of the then few women drivers, a fierce proto-feminist with a piercing shriek of a voice. As they bounced along the potholed dust-swirling tracks of an embryonic **urbanización** — mostly building site and wasteland — on the outskirts of Jávea, Valerie had no idea that she was rattling around in the vehicle that had helped to start the Spanish Miracle, as the economic recovery after the tough post-Civil War years was called, and one of its most enduring symbols. Look at any photo of any Spanish city from the late 1950s and 1960s and there appears to be no other car on the road. Like the Model T Ford, the dinky Seat 600 (Seiscientos) was a car that became a legend. First made in 1957, this copy of the Fiat 600 was the first mass-produced Spanish car affordable for anyone other than the stinking rich. Getting ordinary Spaniards on the roads en masse, it ushered in a period of major social change. The way Spaniards used their leisure time, and their whole lives, changed, as *turismo* took off. In fact, ordinary private cars came to be called *turismos,* and you can still see this word on road signs, at motorway tolls etc. The Seiscientos is now a cult object, with dedicated websites, Friends of the

Seiscientos clubs all over Spain, and rallies when these robust, roadworthy little cars, lovingly kept in a superb state of repair, are proudly driven forth.

Selectividad Colloquial term for the university entrance exams, officially known as las PAU: Pruebas de Acceso Universitario. Known colloquially as *la Selec* or *la Sele*.

Semana Blanca White week. Two meanings. 1) Special week at your local branch of **El Corte Inglés** when you are urged to buy such items as bed linen, tablecloths, and bath towels at bargain (still higher than anywhere else) prices. 2) Half-term holiday towards the end of February in some autonomous communities. Sacred to teachers and pupils, who already have extremely long holidays. Dreaded by working parents, who don't. In 2001 the education authorities pleased and angered in equal parts when they proposed to suppress "white week" and shorten the Easter, summer and Christmas holidays, thereby adding 20 teaching days to the school calendar.

Semana Santa Easter week or Holy Week. In Spain, this means the week leading UP to Easter, not the week afterwards. While school children still have the whole of Semana Santa off school (including Easter Monday in some autonomous communities), only Jueves Santo and Viernes Santo (Easter Thursday and Good Friday) are public holidays. Nonetheless, judging by the trade done by the travel agencies during this period, some employers regard the week as one giant *puente* and give their workers an extended holiday.

Señor, Señora, Señorita Mr, Mrs and Miss. There's no such thing as Ms in Spanish. Theoretically, you're either young and unmarried (*señorita*) or older and married (*señora*). What happens in practice is that as long as the person (read: male) addressing you deems you young enough and/or good-looking enough, you remain a don't-worry-your-pretty-little-head *señorita*. Go on, protest at the chauvinism of it all, but when all you ever hear is *señora*, you start hoping for the odd fluffy miss.

Señorito Master. A word that conjures up times, thankfully past, of arrogant young aristocrats maltreating and abusing manservants and maids.

Señor Ministro/Señora Ministra. The correct way to address a government minister. We also have Mr or Mrs mayor, director, public prosecutor, as in *Señor* or *Señora alcalde, director/a, fiscal.*

Servicio *El servicio* (or *los servicios*) is the politest way to refer to the lavatory. Not easy to pronounce without a lisp. For the third syllable, take the "th" from think and try this: sair-VEE-thee-oh. *Servicio* also refers to a place setting at a restaurant, but not to a dinner service, which is *una vajilla. Servicio militar* is military service; *servicio doméstico*, domestic service; and *servicio a domicilio*, delivery service (for example, at a supermarket). But while *servicios de urgencias* are emergency services, and *servicios públicos,* public services, customer service is *atención al cliente*, service in tennis is *saque,* and a religious service, *un oficio religioso.* As you might expect, on a bill *servicio* refers to the service charge. At the bottom of one menu it was (mis)translated into English as "Water closets included". We should hope so.

Sidra Not only the patrimony of Somerset, but also Asturias and the Basque country. Served in *sidrerías* throughout the regions, the drink is famously poured, or rather slung, from a great height with one arm outstretched behind the head and the other fully extended below holding the glasses. Sidra de Asturias is one of Spain's **IGP** products.

Siesta What can be said about siesta that you don't already know? Perhaps that it comes from the Latin *"sextear"* or *"guardar la sexta"* as laid down in the Rule written by Saint Benedict in the sixth century. Benedict divided the monastic day into three-hourly periods: Laudes (00.00), Matins (03.00), Prima (06.00), Tertia (09.00), Sexta (12.00), Nona (15.00), Vespers (18.00) and Compline (21.00). After the *sexta hora,* he ruled, monks should rest and remain in silence. The word *sextear* gradually morphed into *"sestear"* or *"guardar la siesta"* and the practice of taking a nap at midday spread into the daily life of Catholic communities around the world. At midday, the Spanish have barely finished their second **desayuno** (breakfast), and, by the time they get round to resting up, the Benedictine monks are well into whatever they do at Nona (15.00).

The correct length for a stretch of *"yoga hispánica"*, as the late great novelist Camilo José Cela once called it, is said to be between 15 minutes and an hour. Any more and the body goes into deep sleep, leaving us feeling **grogui** and unrefreshed on waking (in one such state Theresa switched off the alarm on her brand-new G3 mobile phone, went back to sleep, and woke up to find the phone reposing in a mug of cold tea on the bedside table). Brevity is the key. Surrealist painter Salvador Dalí reputedly took his siestas sitting up, holding a teaspoon in his hand. When the spoon dropped, he woke up, and his nap was over. We've tried it, pen in hand on the sofa. It works.

Sin Not a crime, but a shortened form of *"cerveza sin alcohol"*, alcohol-free beer. Just ask for *"Una sin, por favor"*. *Sin* means without.

Solicitud/solicitar Application/to apply for, or fill in an application form.

Sudaca A slang word referring to a South American. Regarded as racist and derogatory.

Súper The Spanish have a syllable-saving tendency to reduce English names and compound nouns to the first word. For example: Los Rollin' (the Rolling Stones), el Trivial (Trivial Pursuits), and, *el súper* (the supermarket, from *supermercado*). Súper (SOO-pair) is also used to intensify adjectives, as in *superbueno* (very good); *superdivertido* (a lot of fun), *superestresado* (really stressed out). You can even use it on its own, if you don't mind sounding terribly Ab-Fab, to mean great, brilliant, perfect: *"Tu pelo ha quedado súper* (Your hair looks darling)."

171

Taller Workshop, in all senses, and with some specialised meanings, like *talleres gráficos*, a printworks. A *taller de reparación* or *mecánico* is a garage or repair shop, a *taller de escritores* is a writers workshop, a *taller de autoestima* is a self-esteem workshop.

Tarde Afternoon starts somewhere between 2pm and 3pm and lasts until it's dark or until eightish, the run-up to dinner time. *La tarde* overlaps with evening as there are only three divisions in the day, not four as in English. The correct greeting during this time period is *"Buenas tardes"*.

Tasca Cheap bar serving food and drink. Conjures up images of any combination of the following: floors strewn with cigarette butts, olive stones, and prawn heads; behind-the-bar décor of yellowing football flags, ancient bullfighting posters and tacky calendars; rows of dripping wine barrels smelling like rotting apples; ceilings hung with hams, strings of garlic and assorted pots and pans; hard wooden chairs barely big enough for the average-sized bum; room to swing perhaps one very small rodent; and in parts of Andalusia a free *tapa* of cheese/*boquerones en vinagre*/meatballs/Russian salad/spicy sausage/shrivelled up olives with every drink.

Tela Material, cloth, canvas, colloquial term for money. *Tela,* or *tela marinera* (lit. sailcloth), is also used to refer to a task that is long or difficult or problematic. The paperwork involved in buying a house, for example, *tiene tela*, and *Don Quixote*, though fun, at 1072 pages (Penguin, paperback) *tiene mucha tela*. Sometimes you will hear it used in an exclamation, as in

"*¡Vaya tela!* (What a job!/That's one hell of a job!)".

Telefónica Commercial break on TV. Stirring adventure music. Close-up of icebreaker crunching, grinding, slicing through solid ice. Music rises to crescendo. With a great crash, the icebreaker thrusts through into the high seas. At last! Telefónica's monopoly is smashed by this enterprising newcomer, a pioneering, cutting-edge operator. If pigs could fly. Valerie and her family yell and make rude gestures at the TV. Having endured an intermittent Internet connection with this company, Telefónica's main competitor, for several years, they know that the more things change, the more they stay the same.

Trying to outdo your mates with Telefónica horror stories is almost a national sport (one such saga in the now-defunct *Barcelona Business* newspaper was actually entitled Kafkafonica), and our knee-jerk reaction to even the mention of the name is to reach for the Valium and/or rosary beads. Only the other day a friend profusely apologised for his new email address with T***, as if he were confessing to sleeping with the enemy. "Of course everyone in Spain would be more than delighted if they burned to the ground," he said vehemently. "But they do own all the lines — and all the other companies are EVEN WORSE."

A popular slang name is Timofónica (*timo* means con trick, scam). Telefónica has been rightly hauled over the coals for serious customer abuse. So far, however, (cross every crossable body part, burn incense, light votive candles, sacrifice sheep's entrails, you name it) all our worst nightmare scenarios have not been caused by Telefónica but by their competitors. And with competitors like this, they can hardly be worried about losing their monopoly. Believe it or not, your line going dead for weeks may not actually be their fault — one friend of ours found her telephone cable had been chewed through by rats. (By the way, when it is used as the logo or corporate identity of the company, 'Telefonica' is written without its accent).

Terceros In legal contracts, insurance policies and suchlike, this means "third party". So *un seguro de daños a terceros* is third-party insurance. But it's also used in far more vague and colloquial ways to mean "other" or "someone else". Valerie remembers struggling with a translation about relations between EU countries which mentioned *"paises terceros"* — she finally realised it just meant "other (non-EU) countries". *A la tercera va la vencida* is the Spanish (i.e. long-winded, tongue-twisting) way of saying "third time lucky".

Tertulia In the bar on the corner of Valerie's street, every afternoon around **merienda** time, the same group of local elderly women gather, some from her building. They push a few tables together and talk and talk and talk, making a coffee last all evening. This is a *tertulia.* In the same bar, there's another *tertulia,* of elderly men. The group of mates who huddle together on Monday mornings to post-mortem the weekend's football is a *tertulia*. (*Never* try to do business on a Monday morning.) Originally a literary gathering, a bit like a salon but usually in a public place (i.e. a bar), the *tertulia* is more broadly any same-time, same-place gathering of like-minded people, typical of Spanish cafe society. And the word has been aptly pressed into service to refer to radio and TV talk shows. A member of a *tertulia* is a *contertulio* or a *tertuliano*.

Tíket Like so many anglicisms, the word ticket has been requisitioned for a new meaning in Spanish. *El tíket* is your receipt, the one that comes out of the cash register. It is NOT a ticket to get into a show or sports event (that's an **entrada**) or on to a bus, train or plane (*billete*). To make things more complicated, the word that does sound like a Spanish version of ticket, *etiqueta,* means none of these things: it's a label.

Tío bueno/Tía buena You're walking down the street, a car slows down behind you and the window slides down: *"!Tía buen-aaaaa!"* Depending on your age/mood/die-hard-with-a-vengeance degree of feminism you blush, smile, scowl, swear or ignore. The verbal equivalent of a wolf whistle.

Tío/Tía 1 Uncle and aunt. If you're talking about both of them, you say *tíos.* Your great aunt is your *tía abuela* (literally your grandmother aunt) and your mother or father's brother is your *tío carnal.*

Tío/Tía 2 Colloquial term for "guy" and "girl", as in *"Es un buen tío* (He's a nice bloke)" or *"Es una tía muy lista* (She's a smart woman". Depending on your intonation and intention, it can sound amiable or downright aggressive. *"¿Eh, tío, qué haces?"* for example, could be the way you greet an old friend: "Hello, mate, what you up to?" Or it could sound like a prelude to trouble: "Hey you, unspecified male person that's getting right up my nose, what do you think you're doing?"

Todos los Santos All Saints' Day, on November 1, is a public holiday in Spain, as indeed All Souls' Day, on November 2, used to be. In the Catholic tradition, All Saints was when you prayed for the unnamed saints in heaven, while on All Souls you tried, through prayer and alms-giving, to work a transfer to Heaven for loved ones stuck in Purgatory. Nowadays, Spanish Hallowmas is essentially a time of remembrance for the dead, when people visit the cemetery to spruce up their family graves, bring flowers, light candles and say prayers. En masse. Tailbacks form for miles around city cemeteries, the traffic police are out in force and special buses are put on to cope with the floral frenzy. In Madrid, about one million people visit the city's 22 cemeteries over the two-day period, and florists do more business than at any other time of the year, including Mother's Day and Valentine's Day.

Bakeries also do a roaring trade because no Spanish festival, solemn or otherwise, is without its own selection of seasonal — and in this case cannibalistic — *dulces* (sweet things). Like *huesos de santo,* marzipan "bones" filled with sweetened egg yolk, and *buñuelos,* fried baby doughnuts filled with cream or chocolate. According to tradition, for every *buñuelo* eaten a soul is rescued from Purgatory, while snacking on a holy bone or two shows that you are not afraid of the dead. There are plenty of regional specialities too, like *panellets* (tiny marzipan cakes) in Catalonia, *arrope* (grape syrup) in Murcia, and roasted chestnuts and yams throughout the north of Spain. The traditional All Saints' Day dish in Jaén is *gachas*, a staple flour-and-water gruel sweetened with milk and honey or sugar. Children in some villages apparently still have fun with the leftovers, glueing up keyholes to keep out wandering souls.

177

Top manta "*Manta*" is blanket and "top" is top. Put the two together and you have the expression coined in the 1990s to refer to the sale of pirated CDs and DVDs in the street. Spain ranks ninth in the world in the sales of pirated CDs and DVDs and the only European country to make the Top Ten. The vendors, mostly immigrants working for local mafias, spread the disks out on a blanket or sheet on the ground, hence the expression. In 2005 the police finally started to crack down on the blanket trade, and many sellers have swapped their *mantas* for *mochilas* (rucksacks). They have joined the Chinese rose-sellers, Moroccan rug-traders and African vendors of sleek wood carvings who ply their wares from bar to bar. Neither the bar-owners nor the customers mind. Only the record industry. The black market value of pirated CDs in 2004 in Spain was estimated at 62 million euros.

Tráfico The Traffic Department: Dirección General del Tráfico (DGT) The capital of each province has its own Jefatura Provincial de Tráfico, referred to affectionately as Tráfico. Like all government departments "serving" the public, Tráfico is characterised by a complicated queuing and take-a-number system, whereby you spend half an hour in the wrong line until you realise you should be in one that's even longer. On the plus side, providing you have all the right bits of paper (you won't — remember the One Thing Missing Law), you can actually obtain, update or renew your Spanish driver's licence in one morning.

Transición *La transición española* refers to the process whereby Spain made the transition from the dictatorship of General Franco to parliamentary democracy. The generally accepted dates that mark the beginning and end of the *transición* are November 20, 1975 (when Franco died) and October 28, 1982, when the PSOE (Spanish Socialist Party) won an absolute majority in the general election. The heady years of the *transición* saw the restoration of the Bourbon monarchy in the person of Juan Carlos, the drawing up and approval of the Constitution (1978), and the (re)birth of the España de las Autonomías. Valerie's most vivid memory is of the festive exuberance of the first elections — the first-ever for several generations of Spaniards — in June 1977. At last! Every surface was plastered with posters, the streets of cities, towns and villages were awash with leaflets. The only topic of conversation anywhere was politics. It was awesome.

Tuna Not a large fish, but a wandering band of student minstrels that keeps alive, almost unchanged, a tradition dating back to the 13th century. Amazing, in these digital days, how many of Spain's future lawyers and doctors, architects, engineers and other pillars of society still prance around in velvet bloomers and beribboned capes, singing "typical espanish" songs, serenading women under balconies and getting buckets of water sloshed

over them by sleepless neighbours. Women and tourists love them, men hate them. Their legendary ladykiller skills trigger barely concealed envy. "This guy in black stockings pulls all the girls," ordinary geeks complain. It all started in Palencia, where the first *studium generale*, the forerunner of the university, was founded in 1212. Young men flocked there, and those too poor to pay their way busked in inns, taverns and medieval greasy spoons for a few coins and a bowl of soup. When night fell and the curfew sounded, they wandered around town, strumming their lutes, singing popular songs under women's balconies and raising hell. Since then, essentially, nothing has changed, and every university faculty has its *tuna*. It is one of the signal achievements of the Spanish to have made the medieval freeloading minstrel life into an institution and, moreover, to have exported it (recently) not only to the rest of the Spanish-speaking world (Portugal has its own version) but to France, Belgium, Germany, Holland and Japan. Foreign tunas, of course, sing in Spanish. Believe it or not, the *tuna* is not just about wine, women and song. It is really a fraternity, they say. Like other male institutions, at its best it's about unfashionable stuff like discipline, commitment, companionship, loyalty, honour, character building. Perhaps this is why it has endured.

Turrón Nougat from Spain? Almond honey brittle? There's no really good way to translate *turrón*, the stuff that Spaniards eat thousands of tons of every Christmas, because it's an experience. There's the melting coconut variety, creamy marzipan studded with bright gems of candied fruit, melt-in-the-mouth egg yolk caramel, or the coveted chocolate-orange dream that sells out weeks before Christmas. However, only the soft *turrón de Jijona* and the hard *turrón de Alicante* qualify for the **Indicación Geográfica Protegida**. Prize quality products of the Comunitat Valenciana, both are made of locally grown sweet almonds and honey. The one thing all true *turrón* has in common is that it is made by traditional methods with natural raw materials of the finest quality. Every year brings new concoctions (aberrations say the purists) like chocolate and kiwi, pineapple praline, Irish coffee, tiramisu, rum'n'raisin, cheese and blueberry praline, *yogu-fresa*, white chocolate.

180

Like vintage wine, a little of the really superb *turrón* goes a long long way. Serve a selection cut into small cubes and savour every bite. Do check out your health insurance for dental cover before even looking at the Alicante, though. Valerie's most abiding image of the Catalan country Christmas is of her father-in-law draped in an old mac, a **Corte Inglés** bag on his head, purposefully squelching across the garden in the sleet to the toolshed and returning to the feast with a hammer and chisel.

TVE Televisión Española, the state-owned television company. Viewers pay no licence, but must endure commercial breaks that last longer than some of the programmes. Despite various reforms, the company still can't quite shake off the legacy of the Franco years when it was subject to tight government control and censorship — and, whoever is in power, its critics always claim that the news is biased (in the government's favour). The first channel, TVE1, flickered into life in 1956, with programming that seemed to consist largely of broadcasts of Franco inaugurating things. In the mid-60s TVE2 (La Dos) was launched, although it wasn't until Spain hosted the World Cup in 1982 that this became available to most viewers. In 1980s the TV network was overhauled and television channels in the autonomous communities started to spring up. Amazingly, though, it wasn't until the end of the decade that the state's monopoly on network links ended and Spain finally acquired three more national stations: Antena 3, Tele 5 and Canal Plus (a pay channel). For years TVE1 could count on the largest number of viewers nationwide, but competition, not least of all from the regional channels, has beaten them down to third place. TVE2, the least low-brow of all the national channels, is still the least-watched by a long chalk. When people who claim not to watch the box are asked about their viewing habits, they say things like: "Oh, I only watch the news and the documentaries on La Dos." Right.

Urbanización We could just be lazy and say "urbanisation". Partly because the usual translation "housing estate" doesn't convey quite the right meaning. For a start, an *urbanización* consists of houses rather than flats making them sound posher than (council) estates. And many are, with communal pools and tennis courts. Some are gated communities, with their own **portero** (caretaker/doorman), security guards, and maintenance team.

Urgencias The Spanish version of a famous TV series that undoubtedly bears little resemblance to reality (okay, we confess: we have never seen it). To judge by local soap operas, *urgencias* is one of the most overused and abused services in Spain today. The baby sneezed: *ia urgencias!* I dropped a five-kilo jar of pickled cucumbers on my foot: *ia urgencias*! Valerie's experience of *urgencias* at Barcelona's Hospital Clinic was, quite frankly, a nightmare. When Enric collapsed at the Barcelona-Liverpool match and was rushed there by ambulance, she sat on a plastic chair ALL NIGHT, along with hundreds of other distraught relatives. The following morning she was finally allowed into the emergency room to find stretchers sardined in there every which way, nurses yelling at distraught relatives as they negotiated the obstacle course to reach their loved ones. It was absolute chaos and an experience Valerie would not wish on her worst enemy.

Usted The formal, polite word for "you" (in writing abbreviated to *Vd* and *Ud*) as opposed to the informal, familiar *"tú"*. *Usted* is used to show respect, to strangers, the elderly, and those in positions of authority. *Tú* is used for relatives, friends, children, pets, pests, vehicles, computers and other unruly appliances. If uttered inappropriately, it could give offence or the wrong impression (if you're a male talking to a female you don't know, for example). But gaffes made by the obviously foreign are usually treated with tolerance. The *tú/Vd* distinction is now breaking down in colloquial speech, but your best bet is still to follow the classic rules, perfectly exemplified in dubbed films. In *French Kiss* for example, Meg Ryan and Kevin Kline meet on a plane and call each other *Vd* until after the first kiss. To address more than one person formally, use the plural *ustedes* (*Vds, Uds*). The usages are different in other Spanish-speaking countries so, if you're heading that way, check them out. A bit complicated? Maybe. But remember that when someone addresses you as *usted*, what they're really saying is *Vuestra Merced* (Your Worship).

Usuario User. There are no longer such things as patients in the health service, only *usuarios* and *usuarias*. *"Paciente"* is apparently no longer politically correct, although it is certainly more accurate in its original sense (a Latin word meaning "suffering") to describe those poor sods who have things done to them by the medical establishment. But nothing has really changed. There's no real Spanish equivalent of "user-friendly". As you will have realised from your daily struggles with DVD instruction manuals, call centres and the assembly of Ikea furniture, the *usuario* is still always wrong.

Utilitario. Small, crappy, we mean economical, car.

Uvas Grapes. We sing *Auld Lang Syne* and hold hands, the Spanish eat 12 lucky grapes. This New Year's Eve custom must date back to ancient times, you may imagine. Wrong: it was dreamed up by Valencia grape-growers in 1909 as a way of off-loading an extra-bumper crop. One grape after each chime at midnight for each month of the year, to give thanks for the past year's good fortune and in anticipation of a prosperous year ahead. A century may be a short time when it comes to gene development, but we're convinced the Spanish have already honed the how-to-eat-12-grapes-in-12-seconds-without-choking gene. Actually, they cheat. The Puerta del Sol clock in Madrid, which everybody watches on TV, is slowed down to a more digestible one strike every three seconds. In 1996, however, even the most adept swallowers came unstuck when it speeded up unexpectedly, leaving half of Spain doing a *Cool Hand Luke* (remember Paul Newman and those eggs?).

UVI Pronounced OOvee and short for Unidad de Vigilancia Intensiva: intensive care unit.

185

V Uve, the 23rd letter of the alphabet, pronounced OObay. One sound that is berry berry hard for Spanish students of English is our letter "v". Volleyball is birtually impossible, and either comes out as bolleybol, or volleyvol. This is because in Spanish both "b" (bay) and "v" (ubay) are pronounced like the hard "b" in butter, best and berry. Thus *vino* is *bino*, *vaso* is *baso* and Vicks VapoRub is **Bikbaparoob** (q.v.). Just to confuse things, when "v" falls in the middle of the word, it is pronounced with a slight, soft vibration, like a "b" but without completely closing the lips.

187

Vacas Ostensibly, cows. However, also part of the new oh-it's-such-a-long-word-do-I-really-have-to-say-it-all shorthand. Save three syllables and enjoy your *vacas*, i.e, your *vacaciones* (ba-ka-thee-YON-es). We blame text messaging. Incidentally, car roof racks are pronounced exactly the same, but spelt *bacas*.

Vale *Vale* of course means "okay" and is one of the first words foreigners pick up. We should be grateful to peninsular Spanish for keeping this word, when almost everyone else, it seems, including Latin Americans and Italians, now boringly say "okay", or rather "ockkay". *Un vale* is a voucher or credit note.

Valencià According to Valencia's Statute of Autonomy of 1982, *valencià* (pronounced 'valenciÁ' with the stress on the final 'a', and called *valenciano* in Spanish) is the language of the Comunitat Valenciana, where it is co-official with **castellano** (Spanish). It is spoken by two million people there and in part of Murcia. There's not much more you can really say about it without getting into extremely deep, complex and emotionally charged waters. Catalan and Valencian are very similar, but Valencian nationalists violently object to their language being considered a variety of Catalan, which they regard as a statement of Catalan imperialism. We could equally say that Catalan is a variety of Valencian. Let's try again. Linguistically speaking — meaning, one hopes, scientifically, objectively, neutrally — Catalan and Valencian, each of which covers a broad continuum of regional variants and dialects, are varieties of one language, which Catalans call *català* and Valencians call *valencià* (and Balearic people call, not unlogically, *balear*). Many Valencians claim or believe that Valencian is a distinct language with a distinct origin, a view which has been promoted for political purposes. While in terms of historical linguistics they haven't really got a leg to stand on, by social, historical and cultural criteria Valencian may certainly be classed as a language in its own right, with its own grammar and spelling rules, school text books and so on. Like British and American English, Catalan and Valencian are mutually intelligible — most of the time.

Vasco Basque. The País Vasco is the Basque Country. The Basque language is called **euskera**

Velocidad máxima The maximum speed limit is 120kmh on **autopistas** and **autovías**. Stick to it and be prepared for all but clapped out *trastos* (piles of junk) to overtake you. In a recent survey by the Spanish RAC, nearly 70 per cent of drivers said they regularly drive over the speed limit. The other 30 per cent were lying. Excess and inappropriate speed causes over 23 per cent of all accidents on Spanish roads.

Ventanilla The *ventanilla* is a great bureaucratic institution. Its function: to slam down in your face when you finally get to a counter after a gruelling stint in a queue. Many government departments, post offices and banks, in order to present literally a more human face, have done away with *ventanillas* in favour of open-plan offices. But this is far, far worse, as the sight of dozens of empty desks with numbers flashing plaintively over them makes you feel even more helpless.

Veranear To spend your holidays somewhere other than where you normally live. From *verano*, meaning summer. For many Spaniards this means moving lock, stock and barrel 10 kilometres down the road either to a rented apartment or a second home in a seaside town, or swapping the comforts of modern apartment living for a falling-apart country *finca* with lots of character, woodworm and damp.

189

Villancicos Christmas carols. Theresa will never forget her first Christmas in Spain, in Córdoba with Francisco's **familia numerosa**. "Before we have dinner," explained Francisco, "we sing carols around the family *belén*." *El Belén* is a Christmas nativity scene made with bits of grass, papier-mâché, and an assortment of biblical figures from the 100-peseta shops. It sprawls on a large table on a covered balcony. About 25 people cram into the tiny space. Forget solemn. Forget reverent. Think hand-clapping, foot-stomping, pub-type sing-alongs and you've captured the essence of Spanish carol-singing — at least in the **García** household. Someone hands Theresa an empty anisette bottle and a fork. Everyone starts banging on a medley

V
Ventanilla
Vacas
Vasco
Vent
lencia
Vale
Ventanilla
V
Vasco
Vacas
Ventanillo
encia

of home-made instruments, bottles and items of cutlery, mortars and pestles, paper combs, jars of lentils and chick peas, and a weird drum-type thing with a stick through the middle (a *zambomba*, she is told). As for the carols, most were lively upbeat numbers, and, from what she could make out, sang the praises of girls called María, the arrival of La Noche Buena (Christmas Eve), and the birth of baby Jesus. Probably the catchiest of all was the one about the frisky fishes: *"Mira como beben los peces en el río/Pero mira como beben los peces en el río/Beben y beben y vuelven a beber/Los peces en el río/Por ver a Diós nacer.* (Look how the fishes are drinking in the river/But LOOK how the fishes are drinking in the river/They drink and they drink and they drink one more time/The fishes in the river, on seeing that God is born)." The **Garcías** even sang one verse in Theresa's honour, substituting "drinkin'" for each "*beben*".

Vuelva Vd mañana Come back tomorrow. The final lethal weapon in the armoury of all Spanish bureaucrats, closely related to the Law of Falta Uno (there's always one thing missing - see **burocracia**)

190

W Pronounced oo-bay-DOB-lay, the 24th letter of the alphabet. Only used in words of foreign origin (whisky, Washington, windsurf, George W.).

Walkmans Or rather "Gwalmans". In addition to acquiring an unrecognisable spoken form, that utterly wonderful invention the Walkman has become plural in Spanish. Valerie once took hers in for repair and when she phoned to see if "el Walkman" was ready, they didn't understand her. She felt really silly saying "los Gwalmans", but it did the trick. As far as the plural is concerned, we have always assumed it was an analogy with *cascos* (headphones), *auriculares* (earphones), and *gafas* (glasses).

Wáter Loo. Yet another of those ill-adapted English words (from water closet). But don't think you will avoid wetting yourself in public by rolling your eyes, clutching your crotch and gasping: "Water! Water!" It's pronounced "BATT-air."

Wifi You won't get anywhere unless you think of a little Scottish married lady. Say "wee-fee". The Spanish word for wireless, by the way, is *inalámbrico* (lit. without wires).

www And you thought double-u, double-u, double-u took a long time to say. To save time when giving web addresses, try this: *tres oo-bay-DOB-lays* (three w's).

19

www   Wáter   W   Wáter
lkmans   Walkmans   www   Wifi   www
www   Wifi   w

X The letter x (ekis) is pronounced "ks" or "s" (*axila, explicar*), and "s" at the beginning of words, mostly in words of Greek origin (*xenofobia, axioma*) or Mexican (*xocoyote*). But there are lots of x-words in *catalán*, *valenciano* and *gallego*. While the sight of them on maps, signs and menus tends to freak people out, they're really easy to say: x is pronounced "sh" (or "ch"). So that ubiquitous institution in Catalonia, la Caixa, is pronounced as "la kasha" (rhyming with Sasha) by Catalans (Spanish-speakers pronounce it "kyesha"); Rianxeira (a make of canned tuna) is ReeanSHAYra. Much easier than Spanish j (pronounced like the "ch" in loch), which replaces the x in the Castilian version of some place names, e.g. Xàbia/Jávea, Xixona/Jijona. Other times, the Catalan-Valencian x corresponds to the Spanish-English-international ch: Elx/Elche, *xocolata*/chocolate, Xina/China. No prizes for figuring out these: Xile, *xat, xip, xampú*. By the way, in Spanish X-rays are *rayos X* (rye-os EKkees), and if you've done something n times you've done it *ekis veces*.

Xunta The Xunta (shoonta) de Galicia is the name of the Galician autonomous government. *Xunta* is the Galician version of the word *junta* (board, committee), possibly more familiar in the expression *junta militar*.

Yeen-toni You do want to be understood ordering a gin and tonic, don't you?

Yonqui Heroin addict. *Yonki* is how the Spanish say "junkie". This word has been officially accepted into the language by the **Real Academia**, with the relevant adjustment to its spelling.

Z *Theta or seta*, the 27th and last letter of the alphabet. In Castilian, pronounced like the "th" in think, but in Latin America "z" is similar to the "s" in sink. Thus, in Spain, *casa* (house) and *caza* (hunting) are pronounced differently (as a rule), while in Latin America they are pronounced the same.

Zambomba Key instrument for **villancico** (carol-singing) sessions. Basically an upturned bottomless flower-pot with a drum-skin stretched across one end and a hole in the middle through which a pole fits. To produce the instrument's low zam-bom, zam-bom sound the player spits on his or her hand and moves it up and down the pole. That's the theory, at any rate. For the uninitiated, about as easy as making fire by rubbing two wet sticks together.

Zamora Capital of the province of Zamora in the autonomous community of Castilla y León, immortalised in the Rome-wasn't-built-in-a-day expression: *No se ganó Zamora en una hora* (Zamora wasn't won in an hour). In fact, Zamora wasn't won, or beaten, at all. Rather, it was held on to. In 1072, Sancho II (under whom El Cid served) besieged the strategically important city in an attempt to wrest power from his sister, Urraca. During the siege, which lasted seven months, Sancho was killed, and the courage of the inhabitants of Zamora passed into the history books — and the language.

Zapear One way of adopting loan words is to add a typical Spanish suffix to the English root. Thus we have *chatear, flirtear, flashear* — and *zapear*. While the purists at the **Real Academia** have admitted *zapear*, they make no such concessions for *zapping*, preferring the more Spanish-sounding *zapeo*. "A Juanito le encanta el zapeo", although little Johnny is just as likely to love *zapping* or *hacer zapping*.

Zara Since we decided to include Zara in this book, just about everyone in Barcelona seems to be carrying their stuff around in a Zara carrier bag. Zara, as hype-loving journalists have been quick to note, is today's Spanish Empire Upon Which the Sun Never Sets, and its emperor is Amancio Ortega, president of the Inditex group (Zara, Pull and Bear, Bershka, Massimo Dutti, Stradivarius, Oysho, Zara Home, Kiddy´s Class). From a tiny family workshop in Arteixo, near A Coruña, since 1975 Zara has grown to over 1,600 shops in 40 countries, 254 of them in Spain. Customers visit Zara on average 17 times a year (four times a year more than the competition), a great marketing success. One of the great achievements of the company is to have become famous without any advertising. Ever seen a Zara advert? Zara's marketing is embodied in the stores themselves: the best premises, the best locations on the busiest shopping streets. Everything is carefully designed down to the last detail, the decor, the window displays, the staff. Nothing is left to chance. Zara's winning formula consists of giving the public what it wants, at the lowest possible price and in the shortest possible time. Telefónica and Co, take note.

195

ZP Thetta Pay, as he is affectionately, and economically, known: José Luis Rodríguez Zapatero, Spain's Prime Minister. The newspapers may refer to him as ZP but to you it's Señor Presidente.

Zurdo Left-handed. *El Zurdo* is also the name of Picasso's very first engraving, of a picador holding a lance in his left hand. Did Picasso portray him thus because he himself was *zurdo*? According to a website list of famous southpaws, he and such artists as Da Vinci and Michelangelo were all lefthanded. Which is strange, because in the many photographs on record of Picasso at work (painting, cutting, writing, filming), it is clear that he was a regular right-handed sort of chap. Currently, Spain's most famous *zurdo* is tennis phenomenon Rafael Nadal.